English Syntax

An Introduction to Generative Theory

Sungwook Kim

Shinasa

Preface

The purpose of this book is to introduce students of English to the generative theory of English syntax. Needless to say, there have already been numerous other textbooks available for this purpose. Actually, I have used several of them as the textbooks for my English syntax class. Unfortunately, however, I have found them unsatisfactory for either or both of the following reasons. First, they are mostly too voluminous to cover in a semester (= forty-five to forty-eight hours in total) that is allotted to an introductory syntax course. Second, most of them are concerned with a specific version of Chomskyan generative syntax, focusing on inculcating a specific theory upon students. As a teacher of English syntax, I consider it far more important to learn how to make syntactic argumentation than to simply get acquainted with a specific syntactic theory.

However, the above remarks should not be taken to mean that this textbook is wholly original. Instead, I have benefited from reading many previous textbooks. More concretely, I have used the following books as the textbooks for my English syntax course: Akmajian and Heny 1975, Bas Aarts 1997, 2001, Carnie 2002, 2013, Haegeman 1990, 2006, Perlmutter and Soams 1979, and Radford 1988, 2004. Especially, Haegeman's (2006) book *Thinking Syntactically* seemed to me to be closest to the desirable model of a syntax textbook that I had in my mind. Accordingly, following

Haegeman, I have tried throughout this book to show how to make syntactic arguments in conformity with the basic tenets of Chomskyan generative syntax.

As for the contents of the present book, I endeavored to deal with essential aspects of generative syntax, but regrettably, I could not deal with syntactic constraints for space and time reasons. In light of my own experience in teaching English syntax, the period of one semester is insufficient to deal with syntactic constraints as well. Yet I think that syntactic constraints are one of the most important aspects of English syntax. Accordingly, if future revisions of this book allow it, I would like to include them in the new version for students who want to study syntax further.

Now I would like to express my thanks to several people. First of all, I am grateful to the publisher Shinasa. In addition, special thanks go to Ms. Sunkyung Kim for her excellent editorial help. I would also like to thank Professor Timothy Main, who read the final version of the manuscript meticulously, checking every awkward or ungrammatical expression contained in it. Last but not least, I have used the manuscript in my English syntax class for the past two years, and many students have helped me clarify some murky points by asking questions concerning its contents. Hence they also deserve my special thanks.

Contents

English Syntax

An Introduction to Generative Theory

Introduction

0.1 What is (English) syntax?

Syntax is a subfield of **linguistics**, the study of language. Accordingly, in order to understand what syntax is about, we first need to understand what subfields linguistics is composed of. As is well known, every human language consists of two basic elements: one is a set of speech sounds and the other is the meanings that match with the speech sounds.[1)] As a consequence, linguistics as the science of language necessarily includes at least two subfields: one deals with speech sounds and the other investigates linguistic meaning. The former is **phonetics/phonology** and the latter is **semantics**.

Let us start with phonetics and phonology. As stated above, they are commonly concerned with speech sounds. Their difference seems to consist in what aspects of speech sounds they focus on. Phonetics investigates the articulatory and acoustic aspects of speech sounds whereas phonology is concerned with the systematic organization of speech sounds in the brain of a language user. Here let us illustrate some phonetic aspects of the English language.

1) By human language we mean natural language. Thus, sign language, computer language, and language used in logic are excluded. Note also that speech sounds and their meanings correspond to Saussure's (1959) signifier and signified. In some languages, their speech sounds are written by means of their alphabet. However, whereas every language has a set of speech sounds, many languages lack their own alphabetic system. So, language is primarily a spoken form. See Bloomfield 1933.

Of forty or so English **phonemes** (= the smallest units of speech sound), we can take three phonemes as examples.

(1) a. /t/
b. /ɑ/
c. /p/

We can describe the phonetic properties of the three phonemes above as follows, taking into consideration their articulatory characteristics.

(2) a. /t/: consonantal, voiceless, alveolar, stop
b. /ɑ/: vocalic, voiced, back, low, unrounded, lax
c. /p/: consonantal, voiceless, bilabial, stop

Now these three phonemes can be combined in six different ways.

(3) a. /tɑp/
b. /pɑt/
c. /ɑpt/
d. */tpɑ/
e. */ɑtp/
f. */ptɑ/

From the above data we may notice that combinations of more than one phoneme can produce a meaningful unit.[2) 3)] We call the

---

2) Can a single phoneme constitute a morpheme in English? There are several examples: the indefinite article *a*/ə/, the plural suffix *-s* (/s/or/z/), the past tense suffix *-ed* (/d/ or/t/), etc.

3) Why are the strings of phonemes in (3d)-(3f) not acceptable as words? Are they accidental gaps or systematic ones? They are likely to be the latter. Problems like this belong to the domain of phonology.

smallest meaningful unit of language a **morpheme**, and one or more morphemes can form a word. The study of how words are composed of morphemes comprises **morphology**. For instance, the following two words are composed of four morphemes.[4)]

(4) a. uninterestingly = un + interest + ing + ly
b. disambiguation = dis + ambigu + at + ion

At the next level of combination, if more than one word combines with each other, there emerges a **phrase** or a **clause/ sentence**. Here we can exemplify two sentences.

(5) a. John follows Mary.
b. Mary follows John.

Note that the two sentences in (5a) and (5b) consist of the same words. If the meaning of a sentence is determined by its component words alone, the two sentences should have the same meaning, which is obviously not the case. This means that the

---

4) Morphology is not concerned with merely finding out what morphemes a word contains. Instead, it investigates how morphemes are combined to form a word. For instance, the words in (4) are not composed by merely arranging the morphemes from left to right. Rather, there is evidence that only two morphemes are combined at a time. Moreover, in the given instances, the second and third morphemes are combined first, and then the first is combined with the result. Lastly, the remaining morpheme is combined. The easiest way to represent the ways of combination is by using diagrams like the following.

(i)

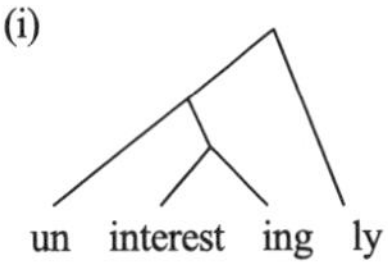

(ii)

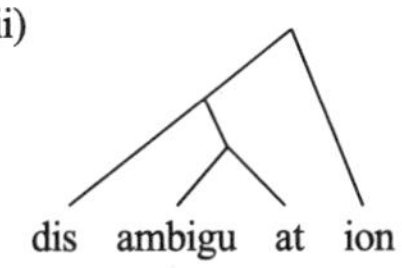

meaning of a sentence is not simply the sum of the meanings of the words used in the sentence. Instead, in order to explain the meaning difference between the two sentences, we have to take into consideration how the words are combined to form a phrase or a sentence. Thus we need to postulate a new subfield of linguistics dealing with the structure of a phrase or a sentence. The relevant subfield is called **syntax**.

At this point, it would be appropriate to illustrate one more concrete example and explicate what syntax is about. We use language to communicate with others, and what we convey in our communication is largely concerned with situational information. Now, let us imagine that the situation depicted in the picture below is happening at the moment.

(6) A situation

How can we describe the situation in English? First of all, we need some relevant words to describe the situation. There is a dog and a cat. The dog is biting the cat. Accordingly, the following words are needed to describe the situation.[5)]

(7) The necessary words: {a, a, dog, cat, bites}

If we can understand what the speaker intends to express by listening to the separate words articulated by him or her, (s)he can be saved the trouble of forming a sentence by arranging those words in an appropriate way. In other words, we need not posit a higher linguistic level than words. Nor need we postulate a new subfield of linguistics. This is to say that phonetics/phonology, morphology, and lexical semantics (= the study of the meanings of words) would do. However, things are not so simple. Since we cannot pronounce the five words simultaneously, we have no choice but to pronounce or write them in a certain order. If every possible order of arranging the relevant words were acceptable, this would imply that word order would be unimportant or insignificant, and any level other than those postulated above would be unnecessary. In reality, however, of the sixty mathematically possible ways of ordering the words in (7), only one is acceptable, as the following illustration shows.

(8) Some possible ways of arrangement of the words[6)]
(the whole possible ways: $(5\times4\times3\times2\times1)\div2 = 60$)
a. **A dog bites a cat.**
b. *Bites a cat a dog.
c. *Dog a bites cat a.

---

5) For ease of discussion, let us describe the situation by use of a simple present tense form of the verb rather than the more appropriate present progressive form.

6) An **asterisk** attached to an expression indicates that it is unacceptable. See (3d-f).

d. *A bites cat a dog.
e. *Cat a dog a bites.
f. *A a bites dog cat.
. . . .

The above illustration proves that in order to express our thoughts, we need to arrange the necessary words appropriately to form a sentence. The appropriate combinations of words to form a sentence constitute the field of **syntax**.

To sum up the above discussion, we arrive at the following (slightly modified) definitions of the subfields of linguistics, which are borrowed from Wikipedia,[7] the famous free-content online encyclopedia.

(9) Subfields of linguistics

Phonetics: the study of the physical properties of speech sounds

Phonology: the study of speech sounds as discrete, abstract elements in the speaker's mind that distinguish meaning

Morphology: the study of internal structures of words

Syntax: the study of how words combine to form grammatical sentences

Semantics: the study of the meanings of words (lexical semantics) and how word meanings combine to form the meanings of sentences[8]

7) *Wikipedia* is blend of *wiki* and *encyclopedia*. The word was coined by Larry Sanger.
8) As a separate subfield of linguistics or a subfield of semantics there is the subfield of pragmatics. **Pragmatics** is concerned with the meanings of sentences in discourse context.

0.2 Why do we study English syntax? (generative syntax vs. traditional grammar)

As you might have already noticed, syntax is not a "new" field of study that has emerged in recent times. Instead, it has a long history of study. Only the term *syntax* referring to the field has been used relatively recently. In other words, **syntax** has almost the same meaning as **grammar**, and **traditional grammarians** had already investigated English grammar for over two hundred years before the study of modern syntax began.[9)]

Thus, you might expect traditional grammarians to have an answer to this question: in order to describe the situation in (6), why should we say (8a), but not any of the others (8b)-(8f)? Traditional grammarians suggest that when we want to make up a sentence, we must see to it that it is in conformity with one of the seven sentence patterns. For instance, in order to describe the situation (6) we should compose a sentence in conformity with sentence pattern III among the seven sentence patterns.[10)]

9) Based upon Pyles and Algeo 1993, let us assume that the study of English grammar began in the year of the publication of Robert Lowth's (1762) *Short Introduction to English Grammar*, which might not be uncontroversial.

10) Arguments for, and illustrations of, the seven sentence patterns can be found in Quirk, *et al.* 1985 and Huddleston and Pullum 2002.

(10) **7 sentence patterns** adopted from **traditional grammar**[11)]

Ⅰ. Subject + Verb
Ⅱ. Subject + Verb + Subject Complement
Ⅲ. Subject + Verb + (Direct) Object
Ⅳ. Subject + Verb + Indirect Object + Direct Object
Ⅴ. Subject + Verb + (Direct) Object + Object Complement
Ⅵ. Subject + Verb + Adverbial Complement
Ⅶ. Subject + Verb + (Direct) Object + Adverbial Complement

A careful observation of the above table reveals that the core of traditional grammar is the classification of sentence patterns, which is based upon the linear order of essential elements of the sentence: **Subject**, **Verb**, **Direct Object**, **Indirect Object**, **Subject Complement**, **Object Complement**, and **Adverbial Complement**.

This seems to be no small feat, since the seven sentence patterns provide the useful templates for forming or analyzing all the basic simple sentences in English. However, this does not mean that the above analysis provided by traditional grammar is flawless. Rather, it has quite a few problems. Let us discuss only some of them so that we can be sure that the advent of a new theory of grammar or syntax should be natural. First, if linear arrangement of words, namely, **word order** is all that matters in sentence formation in English, how can we explain the **ambiguity** of the following

11) Sentence patterns VI and VII are motivated for generating examples like the following.

(i) John lives *(in London).
(ii) John put the book *(on the shelf).

Note that *(XP) means that sentences containing the mark become ungrammatical if XP is omitted.

examples in the light of their word order alone?[12)]

(11) While walking along the street, I saw tall men and women doing Psy's Gangnam Style dance at the square.

(12) London 2012: Black Cab Drivers Protest over Games Lanes Ban (BBC headline)

The sentences in (11)-(12) show that constructing English sentences does not seem to involve merely the linear arrangement of their essential elements. There seems to be more than that. Otherwise, the underlined parts in (11) and (12) would not be ambiguous, because none of the words contained in them is ambiguous. Where then does the ambiguity come from? A careful observation of the data would lead us to conclude that their ambiguity can be attributed to *how words are combined*, not merely to *how they are ordered*. (Note that one word order produces two different meanings!)

(13) The two meanings of *tall men and women*
  a. 'tall men and tall women'
     The meaning results from first combining *men* and *women* by means of *and*, and then modifying the whole with *tall*.

12) A sentence or a phrase can show not only ambiguity attributable to its structure (= structural ambiguity), but also ambiguity due to a certain word contained in it. Observe the following example.

(i) We went to the bank last Wednesday.

The ambiguity of the sentence in (i) results from the ambiguity of the word *bank*. We call this ambiguity lexical ambiguity, as compared with the structural ambiguity discussed in the text.

b. 'women and tall men'

The meaning results from first combining *tall* and *men* and then combining the resultant phrase with *women* by means of *and*.

We can represent how words are combined in two ways. One is to use a pair of brackets to enclose the combined units, and the other is to use lines connecting the combined units.

(14) a. [tall [men and women]]

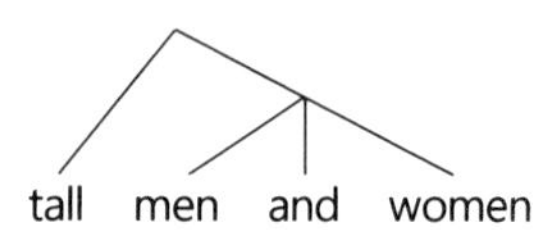

b. [[tall men] and women]

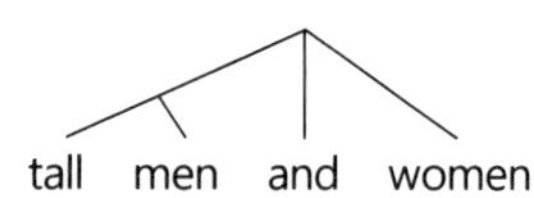

Now if we use these methods of representation, we can account for the ambiguity of the underlined phrase in (12) by the fact that the three words can be combined in two ways.

(15) Disambiguation of *Black Cab Drivers*

a. 'cab drivers who are black'

[black [cab drivers]]

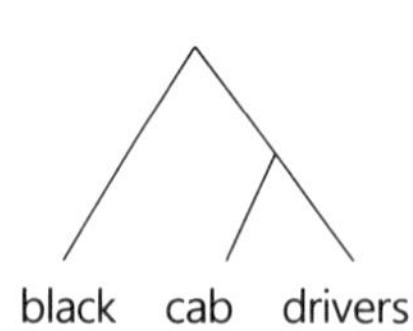

b. 'drivers of black cabs'

[[black cab] drivers]

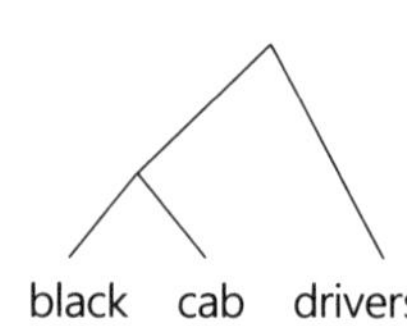

As we showed above, it is evident that grammatical theory

taking into account word order alone cannot account for **structural ambiguity**, a very important property of language.

Next, what about the following pair of examples?

(16) a. John is easy to please.
b. John is eager to please.

If we analyze the above pair in the light of their word order alone, we have no choice but to conclude that they have the same structure: **Subject + *be* + adjective + *to*-infinitive**. In fact, however, despite their superficial similarity, the pair are not quite the same, in view of the fact that they cannot be paraphrased in an identical way, as shown below.

(17) a. It is easy to please John. (= John is easy to please.)
b. *It is eager to please John. (≠ John is eager to please.)

Data like the following also cause problems for traditional accounts, which rely heavily on sentence patterns.[13)]

(18) a. I persuaded him not to stay at my house.
b. I wanted him not to stay at my house.

According to the traditional account, both sentences in (18) have the same structure, that is, belong to the same sentence pattern V: **Subject + Verb + Object + Object Complement (=*not*+*to*-infinitive)**.

13) For detailed discussion on examples like these, see Akmajian and Heny 1975, Postal 1974, and Aarts 1997, 2001.

Since they have the same structure, we expect that they will be interpreted in the same way. In actuality, however, they are quite different in interpretation as the following paraphrases show.

(19) a. I persuaded him that he would not stay at my house.
b. What I wanted was for him not to stay at my house.

The sentence in (18a) implies that I persuaded him, whereas the sentence in (18b) does not imply that I wanted him. In other words, the relationship between the verb *persuaded* and the apparent object *him* is different from that between the verb *wanted* and the apparent object *him*. This shows that sentence patterns based upon the surface word order are not sufficient to account for the syntactic traits of a sentence.

0.3 What are we studying in this English syntax textbook?

Examples like those in (11), (12), (16), and (18) lead us to conclude that we cannot explain some characteristic properties of English sentences by analyzing them in terms of their linear word order alone. Instead, they show that in analyzing a sentence we should consider at the very least which of the words are combined more closely than others. In addition, we should consider how sentences are derived, not merely the superficial surface structure.

Thus, modern syntax tries to explicate two things about the syntactic structure of grammatical sentences: ① how are words combined to form sentences?; ② what syntactic operations are additionally needed to form sentences?

As is well known, the number of possible English sentences is infinite. This does not mean, however, that there are an infinite number of different structures in English, as can be noticed even from the traditional analysis of English sentences. Rather, researchers expect there to be a very simple rule system for forming an infinite number of sentences. Thus, in the present course we will be mainly concerned with these two problems: ① how can we analyze the syntactic structures of the following two sentences?; ② what syntactic operations occur during the course of their derivations?

(20) These students of history will be visiting the museum on Tuesday. (Henceforth, we will call this sentence **the *students* sentence**.)

(21) When do you think that the students of English history will visit the British Museum?

We will deal with the two problems from the perspective of **generative syntax**, founded by Chomsky,[14] not from the perspective

14) Noam Chomsky (1928~) (/noʊm ʧɑmski/) is an American linguist, philosopher, cognitive scientist, logician, political critic, and activist. He is an Institute Professor (Emeritus) in the Department of Linguistics & Philosophy at MIT, where he has worked for over 50 years. In addition to his work in linguistics, he has written on war, politics, and mass media, and is the author of over 100 books. According to the Arts and Humanities Citation Index in 1992, Chomsky was cited as a source more often than any other living scholar from 1980 to 1992, and was the eighth most cited source overall. He has been described as a prominent cultural figure, and he was voted the

of traditional grammar, whose limitations we have indicated above. In the course of analyzing these sentences as well as many more additional sentences you will realize that syntactic structures of English are derived in very systematic and intriguing ways.

Before completing this introduction, let me clarify the term "generative" in Chomskyan generative syntax. As a cognitive linguist, Chomsky asks how native speakers of a language can acquire it so rapidly, that is, within thirty months after birth, and produce and understand an infinite number of sentences without any difficulty. He argues that they can do so because they have innate language faculty to acquire their native language. In addition, the language faculty in their brain/mind is considered to consist of a very simple system of rules for generating an infinite number of sentences. Thus, the main task of syntacticians, Chomsky claims, is to precisely formulate the generative rule system that is believed to be in the brain of a native speaker. Consequently, Chomskyan syntax, which aims to explicate the rule system for generating all and only grammatical sentences, is characterized as "generative." In other words, generative syntax is concerned with finding (simple) algorithms for generating **all and only** grammatical sentences of human language.

Another striking characteristic of Chomskyan generative syntax is that it is scientific. Accordingly, in order to understand

"world's top public intellectual" in a 2005 poll. Chomsky has been described as the "father of modern linguistics" and a major figure of analytic philosophy. His work has influenced fields such as computer science, mathematics, and psychology. (adapted from Wikipedia)

it properly we need to understand what it means for an academic field to be scientific. Briefly speaking, we call an academic field scientific only if it uses scientific methodology. Now, what does scientific methodology involve?

The overall process of scientific research involves **observing** a natural phenomenon (needless to say, language is certainly a sort of natural phenomenon), **asking questions** concerning it, positing **hypotheses** to answer the posited questions to account for the relevant phenomenon, deriving **predictions** from them by logical inferences, and then carrying out **experiments** based on those predictions to determine whether the original hypothesis is correct.

In order to understand scientific methodology, let us imagine a scenario: suppose you were born in England in 1642, and your name is Isaac Newton. As a child interested in natural phenomena, you are lying under an apple tree, enjoying a sunny autumn day. All of a sudden, a fully ripe apple falls to the ground near your head. Now you can study this seemingly simple natural phenomenon by means of scientific methodology, taking the following steps.

Formulating a question: why do apples fall to the ground?

Hypothesis: a hypothesis is an answer to the question which is conjectured based on one's knowledge. Concerning the above question, you may suggest at least four possible hypotheses, each of which is stated below.

(22) Possible hypotheses concerning the formulated question
  a. Hypothesis 1: apples fall because they are fully ripe.
  b. Hypothesis 2: apples fall because they are fruit.
  c. Hypothesis 3: apples fall because autumn has come.
  d. Hypothesis 4: apples fall because of the gravitation of the earth.

Prediction: this step involves determining the logical inferences of a hypothesis. For each of the above hypotheses, we can predict the following.

(23) Prediction from each hypothesis
  a. Prediction from Hypothesis 1: apples that are not fully ripe will not fall.
  b. Prediction from Hypothesis 2: things other than fruit will not fall.
  c. Prediction from Hypothesis 3: apples will not fall before autumn comes.
  d. Prediction from Hypothesis 4: everything will fall if the gravitation of the earth has influence on it and nothing prevents it from falling.

Test: this is an investigation of whether the real world behaves as predicted by the hypothesis. If necessary, scientists test hypotheses by conducting experiments. How can you test the four hypotheses?

Data extension and a new hypothesis: if a hypothesis is proved to have some explanatory power, then the scientist collects more data related to the formulated question, and in due course he or she is likely to pose further questions *ad infinitum*.

In actuality, based upon his observations and scientific research concerning the posed question, Newton finally reaches and formalizes his law of universal gravitation as follows.

(24) Newton's law of universal gravitation
Any two bodies in the universe attract each other with a force that is directly proportional to the product of their masses and inversely proportional to the square of the distance between them.

$$F_{grav} \propto \frac{m_1 \times m_2}{d^2}$$

In this book I hope you will become acquainted with the precise meaning of scientific methodology applied to syntactic study.

Taking this general introduction as a background, we will start our syntactic study in the next chapter. It will be mainly concerned with discussion of general properties of words, the smallest components of the sentence.

Exercise 1 The following expressions are ambiguous. State where the ambiguity comes from. In addition, for each reading, provide a paraphrase that is itself unambiguous.

(1) a. My dog was carrying a mouse in his mouth.
    b. His pupils are moving actively.
    c. John may go home right away.

(2) a. chocolate cake icing
    b. clever boys and girls
    c. Writing clearly is important. (Greenbaum and Nelson 2009:153)
    d. He said on several occasions he suffered from headache. (*ibid.*:152)
    e. They should decide if they will come tomorrow.

Exercise 2 Discuss the interpretation of the underlined parts in the following examples, and point out some difficulties that the analysis based upon sentence patterns may face.

(1) Putin ordered the diplomats to do as much as possible to force the conflicting sides to reach a peaceful political solution <u>on July 9</u>. (*Time*, July 23, 2012)

(2) a. Tony believed <u>Lewis</u>.
    b. Tony believed <u>Lewis</u> to be dishonest.

(3) a. Bill preferred <u>his son</u> to abandon the project.
    b. Bill forced <u>his son</u> to abandon the project.

Chapter 1 Word Classes

1.1 What are word classes?

Given the definition of syntax, i.e., the study of how words are combined to form a grammatical sentence, words are the building blocks of syntax. Therefore we start syntactic study by analyzing words. We can analyze words largely in two ways. One is to analyze their internal structure, which comprises **morphology**, a field of linguistics separate from syntax. The other is to classify words into groups based upon their characteristic properties. From the perspective of syntax, the latter is very important, for, as will become clear in the following discussion, combinatory capabilities of a word are determined by what word group it belongs to. We call these groups **word classes**.[15)]

As an exercise, let us classify the following words.

(1) *dog, happy, drive, sharply, or, upon, they, the*

Each word belongs (∋) to a certain category, as shown below.[16)]

---

15) The traditional term corresponding to word classes is **parts of speech**. The latter does not seem to be very felicitous as pointed out by Jespersen (1933:66). Accordingly, we adopt the term **word classes** or **lexical categories** instead.

16) Note that the two words *dog* and *drive* can also be used as a verb and a noun, respectively. One of the most idiosyncratic properties of English is that one word can be used as various word classes.

(2) *dog* ∋ noun, *happy* ∋ adjective, *drive* ∋ verb, *sharply* ∋ adverb, *or* ∋ conjunction, *upon* ∋ preposition, *they* ∋ pronoun, *the* ∋ determiner

How can native speakers of English (as well as you) identify the word class of each word? In their brain/mind there must be **some criteria** for the classification of words or the **definitions** of word classes. Can we state them **explicitly**?

1.2 How can we define word classes?

As can be found in many English grammar books, there have been three definitions of word classes suggested. It goes without saying that the kind of definition depends upon the criterion used to classify words.

A. **Semantic** definition

The first definition is based upon the **meanings** of words. Thus, the category of a word is considered to be determined by its meaning. For instance, we can provide the semantic definitions of nouns, verbs, and adjectives as follows.

① **Nouns** are words naming **people**, **things**, or **places**.

(3) *Thomas, lady, John, apple, bear, school, sky, playground, Korea, ...*

② **Verbs** are words describing **actions** or **activities**.

(4) *kick, hit, run, swim, speak, work, study, fly, ...*

③ **Adjectives** are words denoting **properties** of people or things.

(5) *beautiful, generous, large, round, slim, fast, strange, valuable, ...*

Discussion 1. Evaluate the above definitions.

B. Formal definition

If we observe words used in a sentence carefully, we will notice that different words exhibit different **forms**. Thus, formal definitions consider the formal characteristics of words in classifying them. Observe the data given below, and try to answer the following questions.

① Can you point out some formal properties of nouns?

(6) *agraffes, caciques, indigenization, laxativeness, natality*

② What can you point out as the formal characteristics of adjectives?

(7) *persuasible, pruriginous, squeamish, happy, kind, ...*

③ What are the formal properties of conjunctions?

(8) *and, or, but, since, after, that, before, because, ...*

Discussion 2. Evaluate the validity of the formal criteria presumed to apply to the data in (6)-(8).

C. **Distributional** definition

As we can see from the discussion (Discussion 2) of the formal criteria, they cannot be used to differentiate all word classes. (Notice that prepositions and conjunctions cannot be differentiated formally, because they have no positive formal characteristics.) The last criterion for classifying words is their **distribution**. On a distributional definition, the category of a word is determined by its distributions in a phrase or sentence. As an illustration, observe the following sentences.

(9) a. The car runs {*fast/swiftly/slowly*}.
    b. This is a very {*fast/expensive/famous/eco-friendly*} car.

We classify the italicized words in (9a) as adverbs. Our classification is based upon their occurrence immediately behind the intransitive verb. On the other hand, the italicized words in (9b) are classified as adjectives, since they occur immediately before the noun.

Of the three definitions of word classes, the semantic one is less reliable than the other two. Why? In general, scientific research is required to be explicit. Linguistics as science also must meet this requirement. Incidentally, meanings are notoriously difficult to describe explicitly. Accordingly, formal and distributional definitions are preferred to semantic definitions in linguistics. For this reason, we will mainly use the formal and distributional criteria for defining each word class in this book. Let us turn to some definitional characteristics of each word class.

1.3 Some characteristics of word classes

1.3.1 Nouns (N)

① **Formal** characteristics

The **genitive case** suffix *-'s* and the **plural suffix** *-(e)s* are attachable to nouns. In addition, there are some typical **derivational suffixes**, for instance, *-ness, -tion, -ity, -al,* etc. Observe the following relevant data.

(10) a. *John's, the boy's, children's, dog's, ...*
b. *books, pens, benches, boxes, pianos, ...*
c. *obviousness, disambiguation, unfamiliarity, arrival, revival, ...*

② **Distributional** characteristics

Nouns can occur immediately behind **determiners**. Henceforth let us indicate possible positions of a word class by means of underlines.

(11) a. a/the ______
b. A *pig* is eating potatoes in the *cage*.

In addition, **nouns** can be positioned to take on the **grammatical role** of the **subject, direct object, indirect object,** or **prepositional complement**. Thus, quite interestingly, we can identify the word class of some non-sense words on the basis of their distribution in a sentence, as illustrated below.

(12) a. *Biggiepops* sleep during the day, and wander around at night.
b. I saw large snakes behind *danteekoos*.

③ Subcategories

Nouns can be subclassified in accordance with their additional properties. For instance, while **(referential) nouns** refer to some entities in the world, **pronouns** usually refer to something by being related to nouns, more precisely noun phrases, which are called their **antecedents**. Thus, in this book, pronouns are treated as special cases of nouns, not as a separate word class. Some examples of pronouns are given below.

(13) pronouns
I, you, he/she/it, they, one, this, that, what, which, ...

For subclassification of pronouns, you may refer to virtually any grammar book you might have.

(Referential) Nouns are distinguished into **proper** nouns and **common** nouns, and the latter into **count** and **non-count** nouns. Their classification is based upon the distinctive behavior of each subclass, as evidenced below.

(14)

proper		*John*	*a *John*	**Johns*	*the *John*
common	count	**book*	a *book*	*books*	the *book*
	non-count	*water*	*a *water*	**waters*	the *water*

1.3.2 Verbs (V)

① **Formal** characteristics

Verbs can take **tense-** or **aspect**-related suffixes—the **third person present tense** suffix *-s*, the **past tense** suffix *-ed,* the **past participle** suffix *-en,*[17] and the **present participle** suffix *-ing*. In addition, there are some derivational affixes which indicate that words containing them are verbs. Observe the following data.[18]

(15) a. Three uggs *wugged* the aggs.
 b. The tiggs are *zegging* aggs.

(16) *modernize, signify, alternate, encourage, widen, ...*

② **Distributional** characteristics

We can detect verbs by considering their distribution in a sentence. Thus, words that can be placed in the underlined part of the following frame are verbs.

(17) Subject _____.

---

17) With most verbs, the past tense form and the past participle form are identical. However, with quite a few verbs, the two forms are different, for instance, *eat-ate-eaten, drive-drove-driven*. Thus, some syntacticians differentiate the two suffixes as the past tense *-ed* and the past participle *-en*.

18) Note that *wug* and *zeg* are non-sense words but evidently, their category is a verb in view of the fact that they take the verbal inflectional suffixes *-ed*, and *-ing*, respectively.

③ Subcategories

Like nouns, verbs can be subclassified in accordance with their additional properties. First, they can be distinguished into **auxiliary** verbs and **main** verbs, depending upon whether they can act as an **operator**.[19)]

(I) **auxiliary** verbs vs. **main/lexical** verbs

(18) a. *Will* you go there? (*will*: auxiliary (verb))
b. *Went you there? (*go*: main/lexical verb)

(19) a. You *can*not eat it. (*can*: auxiliary)
b. *You *ate* not it. (*eat*: main/lexical verb)

Main/lexical verbs are traditionally distinguished into **intransitive** and **transitive** verbs. The distinction is made according to whether they require an object or not.

(II) **intransitive** verbs vs. **transitive** verbs

(20) a. Bill *runs* every morning. (*run*: intransitive verb)
b. Bill doesn't *like* *(eggs). (*like*: transitive verb)

19) As Palmer (1990) and Aarts (2011) point out, auxiliaries are known to share NICE—an acronym made from N(egation), I(nversion), C(ode), and E(mphasis)—properties. Thus, they can be followed by the negative particle *not*, inverted with the subject in questions, stranded with the rest of the predicate ellipted, and emphasized. When auxiliaries display one or more of the NICE properties by participating in these syntactic processes, they are said to "act as an operator."

1.3.3 Adjectives (A)

① **Formal** characteristics

Adjectives are also distinguished from other word classes by their distinctive formal characteristics. They can usually take the **comparative** (*-er/more*) and the **superlative** (*-est/most*) forms. Derivational suffixes like those in (21b) also indicate that words containing them are adjectives.

(21) a. *rich–richer–richest, important–more important–most important*
b. *attentive, eatable, beautiful, joyous*, ...

② **Distributional** characteristics

The typical position an adjective is located in is between a determiner and a noun, as represented by the following frame.

(22) a(n) ____ N

③ **Subcategories**

Adjectives usually denote properties of an object. Thus, they are mostly **gradable** although it is true that there are quite a few **non-gradable** adjectives.

(I) **gradable** vs. **non-gradable**

(23) a. very/quite/pretty *warm*
b.*very/*quite/*pretty *square* cf. *alive, dead, pregnant, triangular*

In addition, adjectives are used attributively or predicatively, as illustrated below.

(II) **attributive** vs. **predicative**

(24) a. This is a very *old* tree. (attributive use)
b. This tree is very *old.* (predicative use)

1.3.4 Adverbs (Adv)

① **Formal** characteristics

A lot of adverbs are closely related to adjectives semantically as well as formally (more precisely, morphologically). Thus, they can also take the comparative and the superlative forms like adjectives. The suffix *-ly* is the most common as a derivational suffix of adverbs.

(25) a. Mary dances more *beautifully* than Betty.
b. *adequately, properly, usually, slowly,* ...
cf. *friendly, manly, homely, weekly,* ...

② **Distributional** characteristics

Adverbs function as a modifier of an adjective, an adverb, or a verb. This can be represented by the following frames.

(26) ____ A; ____ Adv; ____ V

③ **Subcategories**

Unlike other word classes, adverbs are subclassified according to their meanings. This seems to be accepted because their meaning differences are comparatively clear.

(27) Semantic subclassification of adverbs
  a. **degree** adverbs: *very, greatly, fairly, pretty, quite, ...*
  b. **time** adverbs: *yesterday, tomorrow, then, now, ...*
  c. **manner** adverbs: *carefully, easily, beautifully, awkwardly, suddenly, ...*

1.3.5 Prepositions (P)

① No **formal** characteristics

Prepositions seem to lack any formal characteristics. Rather, the fact that they never change their forms in any context is their "formal" characteristic. Thus, some traditional grammarians called them "indeclinable" words.

② **Distributional** characteristics

Prepositions always require a complement, which is usually expressed by a noun phrase. This can be represented by the following frame.

(28) ________ NP

③ **Subcategories**

Like adverbs, prepositions can be divided into several semantic subgroups.

(29) a. **locational** prepositions: *on* the table, *at* the bus stop, ...
b. **temporal** prepositions: *on* Christmas eve, *during* the summer, ...
c. **metaphorical** prepositions: rely *on* him, talk *about* Holms, ...

1.3.6 Determiners (D)

① No **formal** characteristics

Determiners are also indeclinable except *this* and *that*.

② **Distributional** characteristics

The function of determiners is to "determine" the referential domain of a NP. And their positions are in front of nouns. Thus, the following frame shows the distributional property of determiners.

(30) _____ N

③ **Subcategories**

Determiners are subcategorized, based upon their semantic properties.

(31) a. the **indefinite** article: *a(n)*
b. the **definite** article: *the*
c. **quantifiers**: *some, any, all, both, every, each, ...*

1.3.7 Conjunctions (Conj)

① No **formal** characteristics

Conjunctions belong to the indeclinable categories.

② **Distributional** characteristics

As the following data show, coordinate conjunctions can conjoin only like categories. This can be captured by the frame in (33).

(32) a. walk and run
b. *walk and old
c. on and off
d. *on and run
e. *pens and young
f. pens and notebooks

(33) X**P** _____ X**P** (X = N, A, V, P, Adv, ... ; **P** = phrase)

③ **Subcategories**

Conjunctions can be subcategorized based upon their grammatical functions.

(34) a. **coordinate conjunctions**: *and, or, but*
b. **subordinate conjunctions**: *although, when, because, since, ...*
c. **complementizers (C)**: *that, whether, if, for*

(35) a. I didn't recognize *that* her hair style changed.
b. Did you know *whether/if* he would study abroad?
c. They waited *for* him to send them a reply.

1.4 Lexical categories vs. functional categories

The above-illustrated seven categories can be cross-classified into two groups: **lexical categories** and **functional categories**. Words belonging to lexical categories are likely to have substantial inherent meaning. Thus, when we hear a word of a lexical category, we can imagine a thing, situation, property, etc. expressed by or associated with the word. On the other hand, words belonging to functional categories usually have little inherent meaning.

As an illustration of the contrastive semantic nature of the two categories, we can compare main verbs, which belong to lexical categories, with auxiliary verbs, which are classified as functional categories. With their inherent meanings, the former receive **sentence stress**, and secure **semantic independence**, whereas the latter, having little inherent meaning, receive no sentence stress and cannot be used alone in a sentence.

The two groups are also different in **productivity**. In other words, while lexical categories allow new words to be coined continually, functional categories tend to be limited in their membership. Thus, for each functional category we can make an exhaustive list of the words that belong to it. For instance, there are ten modal auxiliaries all told: *will, shall, can, may, must, would, should, could, might, ought (to)*. Likewise, we can list all the determiners as well as conjunctions. This implies that functional categories are hardly likely to coin new members. Actually, we do not expect that new auxiliary verbs, new determiners, or new conjunctions will be created in the future. By contrast, new nouns, adjectives, verbs, and adverbs are constantly being made and will continue to be.

Now, what about prepositions? In the case of prepositions, these criteria for distinguishing between lexical and functional categories seem to apply rather inconsistently. Thus, most prepositions have antonyms (*in* ↔ *out, on* ↔ *off, above* ↔ *below, up* ↔ *down*, etc.), which supports the view that they can be considered to have inherent meanings, but new prepositions are hardly likely to be made.[20)] Incidentally, prepositions are similar to transitive lexical verbs in that they can take NPs as their object, which also seems to support the notion that they belong to lexical categories. Here, following conventions in current generative syntactic circles, let us assume that prepositions belong to a lexical category.[21)]

To sum up, representative lexical categories are nouns, (main) verbs, adjectives, prepositions, and adverbs, whereas functional categories subsume determiners, conjunctions, and auxiliaries. In this book we treat pronouns as a subcategory of nouns, and therefore let us assume without argument that they belong to a lexical category.

---

20) Can you come up with any other property of prepositions that calls into question that prepositions are lexical rather than functional? The fact that prepositions usually receive no sentence stress may lead us to consider them to be functional rather than lexical.

21) Unlike most other generative linguists, Carnie (2002, 2013) classifies prepositions as functional.

1.5 From words to phrases

If two or more words are combined, or **merged** together,[22)] they form a phrase (and can of course form a clause or even a sentence). As an illustration, we can give examples like the following.

(36) a. two words: *large birds, sing merrily, greatly impressive, very comfortably, in Korea, ...*
b. three words: *on the porch, very harmful acts, walked very carefully, ...*
c. four words: *flowers in the garden, right up the ladder, very proud of himself, ...*

At this point, we need to bear in mind that just as every word is categorized on the basis of its semantic, formal/morphological, and distributional characteristics, so every phrase can be categorized in accordance with its various properties. But the fact that it consists of more than one word seems likely to make categorization of the latter more difficult. For instance, if a word of the category X is combined with a word of the category Y, what is the category of the resulting phrase? Is it X, Y, or a third category Z?

In order to find the answer to this question, let us examine how the category of each phrase in (36) is determined. Our intuitions provide the following categorization without much difficulty.

22) Note that "merge" and "combine" have the same sense, but the former is a more technical term than the latter. So in the current literature "merge" is used instead of "combine."

(37) Noun Phrases (**NP**): *large* ***birds****, very harmful* ***acts, flowers*** *in the garden*
Verb Phrases (**VP**): ***sing*** *merrily,* ***walked*** *very carefully*
Adjective Phrases (**AP**): *greatly* ***impressive,*** *very* ***proud*** *of himself*
Adverb Phrase (**AdvP**): *very* ***comfortably***
Prepositional Phrases (**PP**): ***in*** *Korea,* ***on*** *the porch, right* ***up*** *the ladder*

If you carefully observe the composition of each phrase and its **label,** i.e., NP, VP, etc., you will notice that the category (= label) of each phrase is identical with that of the word in bold type. This means that if two or more words of different categories are merged,[23)] the category of the resulting phrase is determined by one of its component words. Syntacticians call the word determining the category of a phrase the **head** (of the phrase).

Now our question concerning the category of a phrase is changed to: how and on what basis can we identify the head of a phrase? A careful examination of the data in (37) enables us to draw the following conclusion.

(38) The common characteristics of a head
a. The **head** of a phrase is the **semantic core** of the phrase. Thus, if X is the head, the phrase as a whole denotes a kind of X.
ex. *Large birds* denotes a kind of birds, not 'largeness.'
b. The head is the most **essential** for forming the phrase in question.
ex. In the phrase *very proud of himself, proud* is the most essential.

---

23) From a theoretical viewpoint the number of words participating in merging is not limited. However, as we will show in later chapters, all mergers are limited to two elements. In other words, only binary mergers are allowed in language. Consequently, as regards the phrasal category we have only to answer this question: if X and Y are merged, which of the two determines the category of the whole, playing the role of the head?

c. In merging X and Y to form a phrase, if X **requires** Y, then X is the head.
ex. In *in Korea*, *Korea* can form a noun phrase alone, but *in* requires *Korea* if it is to form a prepositional phrase. Hence *in* is the head.

d. In merging X and Y, if X **determines** the form of Y, X is the head.
ex. In PPs like *among them*, the head *among* requires the accusative form (*them*) of its object, disallowing the nominative (**among they*) or genitive form (**among their*). Regarding this phenomenon, a head is said to "**select**" its complement.[24)]

Here it is necessary to keep in mind one important point: even one word can act like a phrase, judging from the fact that it can substitute for a phrase, as illustrated below. Therefore, in syntax, one word used without any modifiers in a sentence is treated as a phrase.

(39) a. {*Large birds/Birds/Children*} are swimming in the river.
b. The sick man {*walked very carefully/walked/ran*}.
c. Tim was {*very proud of his sons/busy/happy/sad*}.

In this chapter we discussed classification of words into several word classes. For each word class we tried to provide formal and distributional characteristics. In addition, we showed that phrases generated by merging two or more words are also categorized and labeled. In the next chapter we deal with phrasal constituents.

24) If X requires Y in merging X and Y, X is the head and Y is referred to as the complement of the head. Thus the term "complement" subsumes (direct and indirect) object, subject complement, object complement, adverbial complement, and prepositional object, all of which are borrowed from traditional grammar.

Exercise 1 Assign a word class to the underlined words in the examples below. Give some arguments for your answers.

(1) Did she eye the two strangers with suspicion?
(2) What do you think of the brown-eyed girl?
(3) Did you get your eye examined?

Exercise 2 State the word class of each underlined word. Provide all the possible arguments for your answer.

(1) I will call you back later.
(2) He carried the load on his back.
(3) But my pride would not allow me to back out now, ...
(Mark Twain, *The Autobiography of Mark Twain*, p. 170)

Exercise 3 State on what grounds you can tell the lexical category of each of the underlined non-sense words.

(1) The yinkish dripner blorked quastofically into the nindin with the pidibs. (Carnie 2002:29, Carnie 2013:46)

What do you think this example implies concerning the three criteria for classifying words?

Exercise 4 Observe the following examples based upon those due to McCawley (1988).

(1) a. Blue is my favorite color.
b. The yellows in van Gogh's paintings are striking.
c. John's shirt is blue.
d. John is wearing the bluest shirt that I have ever seen.

Name the word class of each of the underlined words and give reasons for your classification. Next, consider the following examples.

(2) a. Bill put on a {deep blue/*deeply blue} necktie.
b. In the living room there hung {light blue/*lightly blue} curtains.

In what way are examples in (2a) and (2b) problematic for your answers to the first problem? (cf. Aarts 2001:51-2) In answering this question, try to give argumentation based upon the following additional data.

(3) a. My favorite food is pasta.
b. My favorite color is blue.
c. My shirt is blue.

(4) a. They are mathematics {*student/students}.
b. All my shirts are {blue/*blues}.
c. John's shirt is {long/dirty/yellow/*length/*dirt}.

(5) a. Mandela was a man of great wisdom.
b. Mandela was a {greatly wise/*great wise} man.

(6) a. We had a {*terrible/terribly} cold weather last winter.
b. Bill's shirt is {light/*lightly} brown.
c. That {deep brown/*deeply brown} shirt is mine.

(7) a. Michael is a lightweight. (< light weight)
b. What's there in that {*weight/weighty} box?
c. John Wilkinson was an American professional light weight boxer.

(8) a. This is a fast car.
b. This car runs fast.

(9) a. Deep blue is my favorite color.
b. My chair is deep blue.

Exercise 5 Discuss what is the difference between the two groups of adjectives.

(1) a. {red, diligent, fast, deep, happy}
b. {pregnant, alive, dead, collegiate}

Can you demonstrate their difference explicitly by making up some constructions based upon the adjectives?

Exercise 6 Discuss the category of the underlined words in the following data.

(1) <u>Sorry</u> seems to be the hardest word. (Elton John)

(2) <u>Happy</u> is the man who finds a true friend, and far happier is he who finds that true friend in his wife. (Franz Schubert)

(3) Certainly parents play a crucial role in the lives of individuals who are intellectually <u>gifted</u> or creatively <u>talented</u>. But this role is not one of active instruction, of teaching children skills, ... rather, it is support and encouragement parents give children and the intellectual climate that they create in the home which seem to be the critical factors. (David Elkind)

Chapter 2
Constituents and Constituency Tests

2.1 Two methods of syntactic representation

As we noted earlier, syntax investigates how a well-formed or grammatical sentence is constructed from a set of words. In order to discover the rules for forming grammatical English sentences, we first have to disassemble well-formed sentences. In other words, in a certain sense, we syntacticians are like the first Korean automobile manufacturers who wanted to make their own cars, modeled on an imported car. What did they do to learn how to make cars? First of all, they must have taken apart imported cars and discovered all their parts. In addition, they must have discovered how those parts were assembled.

Back to the work of syntacticians, in order to explicate how a grammatical English sentence is formed, we need to know what its "parts" are and how they are combined. What are the smallest component parts or units of a sentence? Obviously they are words. Accordingly, **syntax** is naturally concerned with **how words are combined to form a grammatical sentence**. As is well known, only appropriate, but not arbitrary, combinations of two or more words result in a grammatical sentence. (Following the current conventions in generative syntax, let us replace the term combine with **merge** hereafter, which has been coined by Chomsky and his colleagues.) Now we can say that grammatical sentences are **generated** by merging two or more words *appropriately*.[25)] What the syntactician should do is precisely explicate what "*appropriately*" means.

Incidentally, where do the words used for forming a sentence come from? Sentences are used for describing some situations. Accordingly, in order to form a sentence, we select appropriate words for describing a particular situation, and we do so from the dictionary we have in our brain, that is, the **"mental" dictionary**. Linguists call the mental dictionary the **lexicon**.

Let us return to the problem mentioned in the paragraph before the last: what are the appropriate ways of merging two or more words selected from the lexicon? For instance, are those (two or more) words merged all at once or are they merged in a step-by-step fashion? According to traditional grammar, words do not directly form a sentence. Instead, they first make up phrases. Then, two or more phrases form a clause or a sentence. This can be summed up as follows.

(1) Syntactic knowledge inherited from traditional grammar
  a. A sentence consists of two or more words.
    Sentence = {word_1 + word_2 (+ word_3 + ... + word_n)}.
  b. **Words** are combined into **phrases**, phrases are combined into one or more **clauses**, and one or more clauses are combined into a **sentence.**

25) Can you give some examples of a sentence consisting of only one word? Should we then revise the statement in the text that a sentence is generated by merging two or more words? You might take examples like "*Stop!*" as a one-word sentence. However, there are several reasons to argue that the sentence contains the understood subject *you*. Accordingly, it does not seem necessary to revise the statement in the text.

{word$_1$ + word$_2$ (+ word$_3$ + ... + word$_n$)} → {phrase$_1$ + phrase$_2$ (+ phrase$_3$ ...)} → {clause$_1$ (+clause$_2$ + clause$_3$ + ...)} → sentence

Just as body, engine, hood, wheel, etc. are collectively called parts of a car, so all the words, phrases, clauses constituting a sentence are collectively referred to as its **constituents**. Note that even the sentence itself is taken to be its constituent. Now the results of a syntactic analysis of a grammatical sentence can be represented as its **syntactic structure**, which can be equated with its **constituent structure**. The syntactic (constituent) structure shows how the smallest constituents of a sentence, namely, the words of a sentence are merged together to form larger constituents, finally producing a grammatical sentence.

(2) Requirements of a syntactic constituent structure
   a. A syntactic constituent structure must show how the smallest constituents (=words) are combined into the intermediate constituents (=phrases).
   b. It must also show how intermediate constituents are combined into the largest constituent (=the clause/sentence).

As a concrete example, let us consider how we can analyze the syntactic structure of the following sentence in (3).

(3) The cat chased the rat.

(4) a. The ***word*** **level** analysis:
   Identification of words and their categorization[26)]

26) Categorization, which was discussed in chapter 1, means classifying words or phrases into several classes and giving corresponding labels to them. Note that "(lexical)

[D The] [N cat] [V chased] [D the] [N rat]

b. The ***phrase*** **level** analysis:
Identification of phrases and their categorization

[NP [D The][N cat]**]**, **[NP** [D the][N rat]**]**
[VP [V chased][NP [D the][N rat]]**]**

c. The ***clause/sentence*** **level** analysis:
Unification of the lower (i.e., word and phrase) level analyses by labeling the whole expression as S or Clause.

[S/Clause [NP [D The][N cat]] [VP [V chased] [NP [D the] [N rat]]]**]**

As we can see from the above examples, the syntactic structure of a sentence can be represented by using pairs of brackets and category labels. More specifically, each constituent is enclosed by a pair of brackets and its category is labeled in (a) small capital letter(s) inside the left bracket. We call this kind of syntactic representation a **labeled bracketing representation**.

An alternative representation is also available. In this representation, every word in an expression is given a category label over it (see (5a)) and a set of upward straight lines starting from a group of words/categories comprising a constituent come together at a single point (see (5b)). The newly formed single point as well as the starting point of each line is called a **node**, and a category label is attached to the new node. Similar processes are continued until we reach the sentence level. An illustration is given

category" and "word class" are equivalent. Following the general conventions in current generative syntax, let us use the term "category" from now on.

below for the sentence in (3).

(5) a.

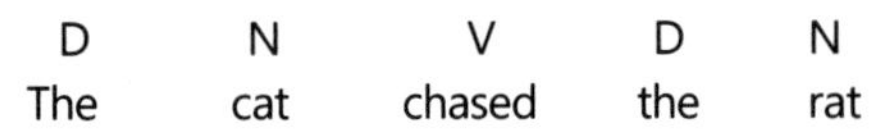

b.

c.

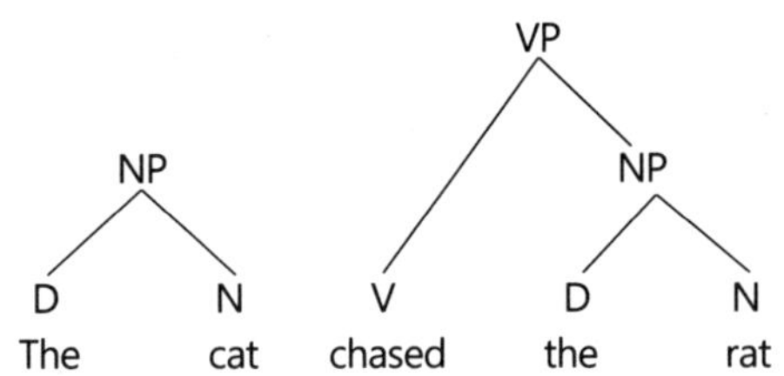

d.

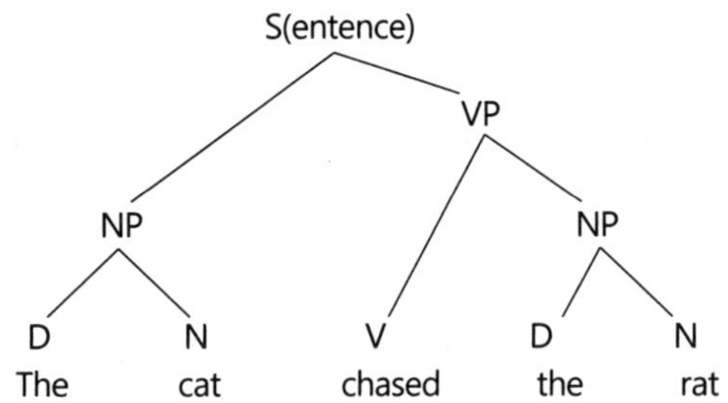

d′.

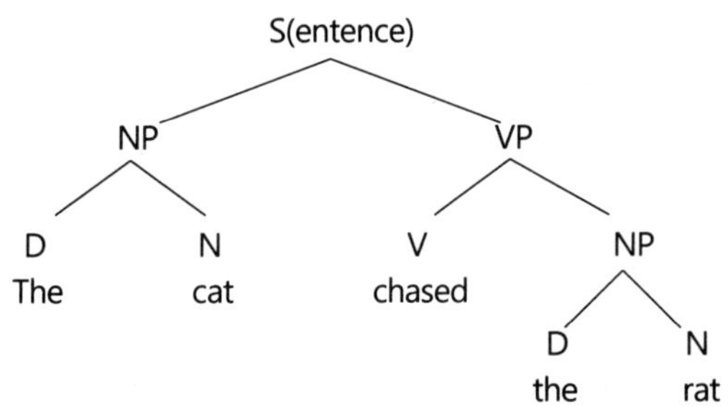

Since we are beginners at this way of representation, we had better get acquainted with it step by step. In (5a) we notice that each word of the sentence is an independent constituent, and therefore it is given a node and its category is labeled on it. In (5b) the lines from *the* and *cat* as well as those from *the* and *rat* are united at the top, which indicates that each pair of words form a new constituent. The categories of the new constituents are labeled on the relevant nodes. In like manner, the verb *chased* and the NP *the rat* are combined into a larger constituent, which is represented by linking the two elements—the verb and the NP—with two lines converging at one point, as can be observed in (5c). The last step of representation is shown in (5d): the two lines from the NP (*the cat*) and from the VP (*chased the rat*) are united at the top, producing the largest constituent, the sentence. The diagram in (5d′) is identical with that in (5d) except that the former is slightly adjusted for aesthetic reasons: the diagram in (5d′) looks more balanced than that in (5d), doesn't it? (If you think that the aesthetic property of a diagram is not important, you need not adjust it in the way shown in (5d′), but most linguists seem to prefer the balanced one.)

If you observe the above diagrams, especially the completed diagrams in (5d) and (5d′), you will notice that they look like inverted trees. Thus, syntacticians dub diagrams like those in (5) **tree diagrams**.[27)]

---

27) The two methods of representation of syntactic structures are completely equivalent from the viewpoint of their informational value. Their difference consists in how convenient they are in practical use: the labeled bracketing representation gets harder

At this point, we have to ask a very important question: how can we justify the above analysis? Why do we not analyze the above sentence like the following?[28)]

(6) a. [The]
b. [[The][cat]]
c. [[[The][cat]][chased]]
d. [[[[The][cat]][chased]][the]]
e. [[[[[The][cat]][chased]][the]][rat]]
f. [[The] [cat] [chased] [the] [rat]]

(7) a. The

b. 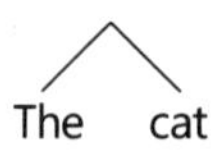

c. 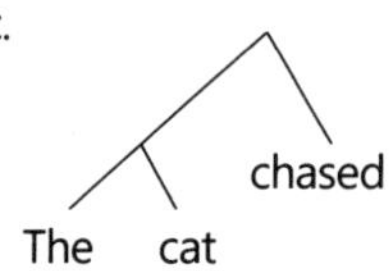

d. 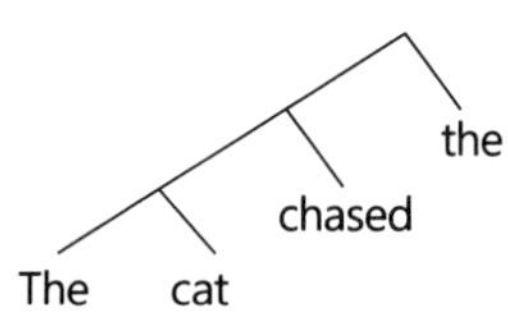

to read if the sentence becomes longer, whereas the tree diagram occupies far more space than the labeled bracketing.

28) From an intuitive viewpoint, the analysis in (6) seems to be fairly plausible, because it reflects the order of writing/pronouncing the words comprising the given sentence.

e.

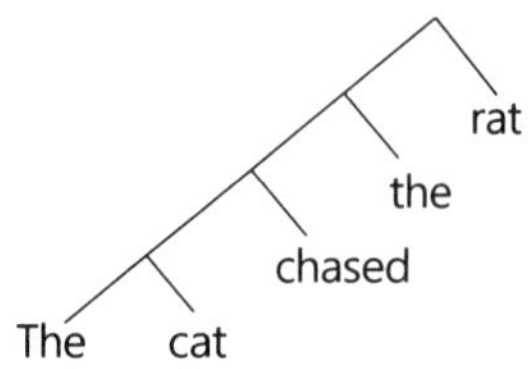

f.

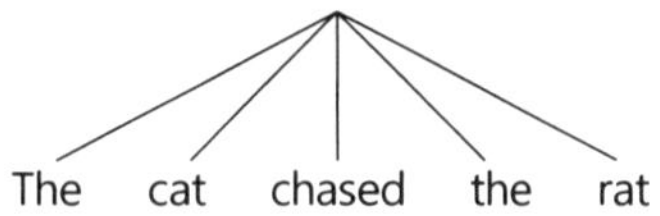

Is their any evidence in support of the analysis in (4c)/(5d, d′) against those in (6e, f)/(7e, f)?

In doing scientific research, we should be careful not to depend too heavily on our intuition. Instead, we should provide as many pieces of evidence as possible that support our analysis. As a concrete historic example, consider the two possible hypotheses for explaining the cycles of day and night observed on our planet.

(8) Hypothesis 1: the sun (or the heavenly bodies) move(s) around the earth.

(9) Hypothesis 2: the earth rotates on its axis.

Intuitively, which do you think seems more plausible? Note that we see the sun rise in the east and set in the west. On the other hand, we do not feel any rotative movement of the earth at all. Naturally, at a glance, Hypothesis 1 seems more plausible. Nevertheless, scientists have proved on the basis of many pieces of evidence that Hypothesis 2 is correct.

What about the study of English syntax? It would be sensible to listen to what Reuland (2011) says about the study of human language. Also we need to bear in mind Radford's remarks quoted below in our attempts to analyze English sentences.

(10) The use of language comes as naturally to us as breathing. This is why it is so tempting to take its properties at face value. A scientific enterprise, however, requires distance from the object of interest, and departing from one's everyday perspective. It starts with curiosity about what appears obvious and natural, and an open mind. (Reuland 2011:1)

(11) ... [T]he structure of a given phrase or sentence cannot be determined on the basis of personal prejudice or pedagogical precepts inculcated into you at secondary school, but rather has to be determined on the basis of syntactic evidence ... I would therefore ask traditionalists to be prepared to be open to new ideas and new analyses ... (Radford 2009:53)

In addition, we need to keep in mind the following steps of scientific research.

(12) **collecting** relevant data → **posing some questions** about the data → formulating a **hypothesis** after careful observations of the given data → **testing the hypothesis** to additional relevant data → **revision** of the earlier hypothesis → ... → **establishment of a theory** of the relevant phenomenon

To recapitulate, since we are trying to analyze syntactic structures of English scientifically, we should justify our analysis as far as we can. Fortunately, with respect to analyses like those demonstrated in (4)-(7), there are several diagnostics that can be used to justify a particular syntactic analysis.

2.2 Six diagnostics for identifying constituents

In the case of the sentence in (3), which is repeated below,

(3) The cat chased the rat.

why do we not analyze it as [[*The*] [*cat chased*] [*the rat*]] or [[*The cat*] [*chased the*] [*rat*]]? The reason is that neither [*cat chased*] nor [*chased the*] forms a syntactic unit (= **constituent**). Now on what grounds do we judge that the two word strings *cat-chased* and *chased-the* do not form constituents? Unlike the word strings *The-cat* and *the-rat*, neither of the two strings of words, namely, *cat-chased* and *chased-the* can be replaced by pro-forms like *it/its, he/his/him, do/do so/do it*, etc. Besides this test, there are at least five more diagnostics for identifying syntactic constituents. Let us introduce and discuss the six diagnostics one by one.

The first diagnostic test for determining constituency is the following.

(13) **Diagnostic Test 1: Substitutability**
If a string of words can be substituted by another (shorter) expression without making the resulting sentence ungrammatical, it is a constituent.

According to the above diagnostic, the underlined strings of words in (14)-(18) are constituents.

(14) Russia, the U.S. and Europe all have major stakes in the Syrian struggle, as ***does*** almost every religious sect and ethnic clan in the Middle east, ... (*Time*, July 23, 2012)

(15) U.S. officials reject the notion that the U.S. is involved in a conflict with ***Russia*** in Syria. Washington is moving more subtly than its old Cold War adversary. (*Time*, July 23, 2012)

(16) In the matter of fifteen-ball pool I never got Dolby's confidence wholly back, though I got ***it*** in other ways and kept ***it*** until his death. (*The Autobiography of Mark Twain*, p. 172)

(17) Thirty years ago a couple of Elmira bankers invited me to play the game of "Quaker" with ***them***. (*ibid.*, p. 173)

(18) The compromise did not appeal to me and I said ***so***. (*ibid.*, p. 194)

The second test for constituency is concerned with movement of a string of words.

(19) **Diagnostic Test 2: Movability**
If a string of words can be moved to another position without making the resultant sentence ungrammatical, it forms a constituent.

The validity of Diagnostic Test 2 can be observed in examples like the following.[29)]

29) Linguistic data fall into two kinds: one is **attested**, and the other is **invented.** Attested data are examples of real language as it has been produced, whereas **invented data** are examples that are intentionally made up by researchers. The examples in (20)-(21) are invented data, while those in (14)-(18), (22)-(23) are attested data. Some linguists prefer

(20) a. The cat chased the rat.
b. The rat was chased by the cat.
c. The rat, the cat chased.

(21) I expected that the cat would chase the rat, and chase the rat the cat did.

(22) How the printers had got hold of her photograph she did not know, but they had, and ... (the British National Corpus)

(23) No one needs to be told this who has read that pathetic and beautiful masterpiece, *Rab and His Friends*.
(*The Autobiography of M.T.*, p. 256)

The sentence in (20b) is formed from that in (20a) by **passivization**: the object *the rat* moves to the subject position of the passive sentence, while the subject *the cat* undergoes movement to the position behind the preposition *by*. In (20c), the object *the rat* has been moved from behind the verb to the pre-subject position. Thus, according to the movability test, *the cat* and *the rat* are constituents. Similarly, the underlined strings of words in (21) and (22) have been obviously moved from the postverbal position to the pre-subject position, showing that each of them forms a constituent. As for (23), the underlined part is a relative clause modifying *No one*, but has been moved to the sentence-final position, which testifies its forming a constituent.

Incidentally, with respect to this diagnostic test, we need to be careful in applying it to data. Let us consider the following set of data.

attested data, claiming that they are more natural and theory-neutral.

(24) a. A: I have read the story about the last Japanese soldier.
B: I have read it too.
b. A: I have read the story about the last Japanese soldier.
B: I know about him too.
c. The story about the last Japanese solder was widely read.
d. *The last Japanese soldier was widely read the story about.
e. ??Who have you read the story about?[30)]

The underlined string of words in (24aA) certainly forms a constituent, since it can be substituted for by the pronoun *it*, as evidenced by (24aB). Likewise, the string of words *the last Japanese soldier* is also taken to form a constituent by the fact that it can be replaced by the pronoun *him* in (24bB). However, this does not guarantee that the string can be freely moved. Instead, it cannot undergo movement in some environments,[31)] as shown in (24d) and (24e).

How can we explain that the two diagnostics do not collaborate? If a string of words can be substituted for by a pro-form, it proves that the string is a constituent (Diagnostic Test 1). Likewise, if a string of words can undergo movement, it also justifies its forming a constituent (Diagnostic Test 2). What must be borne in mind is that with respect to the movability test, the reverse is not true: just because a certain string of words is a constituent

---

30) It is well known that **grammaticality judgement** is not a matter of either grammatical or ungrammatical, but a matter of degree. Thus, *, ?*, ??, and ? are used to represent different degrees of ungrammaticality. The first marks fully ungrammatical expressions, while the last marks marginal expressions. Needless to say, grammatical sentences have no mark attached to them.

31) Following Ross (1967, 1980), syntacticians call the environments out of which some constituents cannot move the **islands**.

does not guarantee that it can be moved. As a matter of fact, movement is known to be restrained by various conditions. So if a string of words undergoes movement, it is sufficient to prove that it is a constituent. On the other hand, the fact that a string of words cannot be moved does not ensure that it does not form a constituent. To recapitulate, movability of a string of words is a sufficient, but not a necessary, condition for proving that it forms a constituent.

Now let us turn to the third diagnostic.

(25) **Diagnostic Test 3: Ellipsis/Deletability**
If a string of words can be wholly deleted in a sentence, it affirms that the string comprises a constituent.

Observe the following examples illustrating the applicability of Diagnostic Test 3.

(26) The cat chased the rat and in the end ø (= the cat) caught it.

(27) I see in other industries there are workers in lighter jobs that are not exposed to the conditions we are exposed to and yet they're entitled to overtime and we are not ø (= entitled to overtime).
(*New York Times*, August 7, 2014)

(28) A good many years afterward ... I would try that anecdote again ... since there would be not a shred of anything in the tale itself that could stir anybody's sense of humor but an idiot's ø (= sense of humor). (*The Autobiography of Mark Twain*, p. 191)

All of these examples commonly contain some elided strings of words, which are taken to form constituents.

The fourth diagnostic relates to *wh*-questions. Although we can characterize *wh*-questions in various ways, one of their prominent properties is that their communicative function is to request some information from the addressee. Thus, the answer the questioner obtains from the addressee constitutes the requested information and usually corresponds to the *wh*-element. This means that answers or responses to *wh*-questions can be considered substitutions for *wh*-elements. Hence, the following diagnostic test can be viewed as a special case of substitutability.

(29) **Diagnostic Test 4: Fragment Responses[32)] to *Wh*-questions**
If a string of words constitutes a fragment response to a *wh*-question, it is a constituent.

Relevant examples are given below.

(30) A: What chased the rat?
B: The cat.

(31) A: What did the cat chase?
B: The rat.

(32) A: When did the Korean War break out?
B: In 1950.

(33) A: Why did he work so hard?
B: For money.

(34) A: How did John welcome you?
B: Very heartily.

32) Griffiths and De Vries (2013) define fragment responses as "nonclausal utterances that can be seen as the remnant of some ellipsis process."

(35) A: Where did you meet your wife for the first time?
B: At Hyde Park station.

The four diagnostics introduced so far are very useful for identifying constituents of a sentence. Still more useful and versatile for identifying constituents is the **Coordination Test**. This diagnostic makes use of the key property of coordination: coordination can conjoin two or more constituents of the same category. In consideration of this, observe the following data.

(36) *Jennifer was pretty and in the room.

(37) *I saw her in the garden and accidentally.

(38) *The old man and suddenly ran toward the car.

The above examples are ungrammatical because the coordinate conjunction (or shortly, coordinator) *and* conjoins two constituents whose categories are not identical. This fact leads us to adopt the following diagnostic.

(39) **Diagnostic Test 5: Coordination**
If a string of words can be coordinated with another string of words, the two strings are constituents of the same category.

Examples showing the applicability of Diagnostic Test 5 are illustrated below.

(40) The cat and the dog chased the rat.

(41) The cat chased the rat and the hen.

(42) Investigations of more than a dozen other banks continued in Continental Europe and across the Atlantic, ... (*Time*, July 23, 2012)

(43) ... the U.S. State Department has worked to establish relationships with opposition groups and is planning to open an office in Istanbul ... (*ibid.*)

(44) Among the larger issues here are why this happened at all, and who are responsible for it.

Note that each pair of the coordinated phrases in (40)-(43) form constituents of the same category. In the case of (44), both the underlined parts have the status of the largest constituent, that is, a clause.

The last diagnostic makes use of two special structures called **cleft** and **pseudo-cleft** constructions. Observe the following triplets carefully, and try to figure out their semantic differences, if any.

(45) a. Billy caught a big turtle on his boat.
b. **It was** a big turtle **that** Billy caught on his boat.
c. **It was** on his boat **that** Billy caught a big turtle.

(46) a. While fishing on his boat, Billy hooked a big turtle.
b. **It was** a big turtle **that** Billy hooked while fishing on his boat.
c. **What** Billy hooked while fishing on his boat **was** a big turtle.

Sentences with the skeletal structure *It is/was ... that ~* are called **cleft** sentences (clefts, in short) and the examples in (45b, c) and (46b) illustrate them. In a cleft sentence, the string of words put into the ... part has the effect of being focused. Needless to say, it must form a constituent, because, in a certain sense, it can be considered to be moved. Similarly, sentences with the skeletal structure *What Subject Verb be* ... are also used to focalize a certain string of words. This time it is placed immediately behind the verb *be* and like focused strings in clefts, must form a constituent. Additional **pseudo-cleft** sentences are illustrated below.

(47) What they need is a good sleep.

(48) What Billy didn't like was the unhappy ending of the novel.

(49) What changed his destiny was a woman he met.

It is well known that in some cases a string of words cannot be placed in the focus position of the cleft even though it is a constituent. This is true, for instance, when the string constitutes a verb phrase, as can be observed in the following data.

(50) a. John wanted to fish in the river last Sunday.
b. It was last Sunday that John wanted to fish in the river.
c. It was in the river that John wanted to fish last Sunday.
d. *It was fish in the river that John wanted to do last Sunday.
e. John wanted to fish in the river and go hiking in the mountains.

Considering that, as shown in (50e), *fish in the river* can be conjoined with *go hiking in the mountains*, it is obviously a constituent, but it cannot pass the clefting test, as shown in (50d). By contrast, the pseudo-cleft construction allows a string of words constituting a verb phrase to be placed in its focus position, as illustrated below.[33)]

(51) What you should do is write an email to the customers.

(52) What I need to do is get some sleep.

(53) What they were doing was arguing about which route to take.

(54) What he couldn't do was sing me a love song.

(55) What I want is to get some sleep.

(56) What he can't stand is getting up early.

From the above observations and discussion, we obtain the following diagnostic.

(57) **Diagnostic Test 6: Focalizability in a Cleft/Pseudo-cleft**
If a string of words can be focused by being placed in the focus position of the cleft/pseudo-cleft construction, the string is a constituent.

33) In order to make up good pseudo-clefts, we need to be careful in using particular forms of the verb located in the focus position (namely, the position immediately behind the verb *be*). Can you draw any generalization concerning the appropriate form of the verb?

2.3 Actual analyses: an illustration

Given the six diagnostics formulated above, let us discuss how we can analyze the following sentence, which looks very simple.

(58) The student of English read *The Great Gatsby* twice.

First of all, we can detect two NPs, *The student of English* and *The Great Gatsby*, based upon several diagnostics, as shown below. (60) represents the two NP constituents.

(59) a. The student of English read *The Great Gatsby* twice. He found it very interesting. (Substitutability)
b. *The Great Gatsby*, the student of English read twice. (Movability)
c. (i) A: Who read *The Great Gatsby* twice?
B: The student of English.
(ii) A: What did the student of English read twice?
B: *The Great Gatsby*. (*Wh*-questions and their responses)
d. The student of English and his sister read *The Great Gatsby* twice. (Coordination)
e. It was the student of English that read *The Great Gatsby* twice. (Cleft)
f. What the student of English read twice was *The Great Gatsby*. (Pseudo-cleft)

(60) [$_{NP}$ The student of English] read [$_{NP}$ *The Great Gatsby*] twice.

At the next stage of analysis, we are confronted with a new task: with which of the two does the verb *read* form a constituent? We can think of the following three possibilities.[34]

34) Can you come up with any other possibilities?

(61) a. [?? [NP The student of English] [V read]] [NP *The Great Gatsby*][35]
b. [NP The student of English] [?? [V read] [NP *The Great Gatsby*]]
c. [S [NP The student of English] [V read] [NP *The Great Gatsby*]]

Which of these three is the correct analysis? Are there any arguments for one against the other two? The six diagnostics can help us provide the answer to this question. Let us put aside (61c), since it is conceivable only when the other two analyses fail. (Combination of three elements seems to be more complex than combination of two, from a cognitive point of view. In addition, a less complicated process is preferred.) What happens if we apply some of the six diagnostics to the sentence in (57), transforming it in several ways? Observe the following data.

(62) The student of English read *The Great Gatsby* twice and so did his friends. (so did = read *The Great Gatsby* / ≠ The student of English read)

(63) The teacher expected that the student of English would read *The Great Gatsby* and read *The Great Gatsby* he did.

(64) The student of English [read *The Great Gatsby*] and [wrote an essay about it].

(65) What the student of English did was read *The Great Gatsby*.

From the results of the above diagnostic tests we conclude that the analysis in (61b) is the correct one.

35) ?? to the right of [indicates that the category of the given constituent is not determined. For simplicity's sake, let us disregard the adverb *twice* here.

In the next chapter we will present further analyses and show that structural analyses of English sentences can be far more complicated.

Exercise 1 Identify as many constituents as possible in the *students* sentence, by using the substitutability test.

(1) These students of history will be visiting the museum on Tuesday.

Exercise 2 In the following pair of sentences the behavior of *these students* is not the same in terms of constituency. Show how they are different.

(1) a. These students will go to Hong Kong next Monday.
b. These students of music will visit the Sydney Opera House.

Exercise 3 In the sentence below the underlined string of words forms a constituent. What is the evidence for such a judgment?

(1) I was in an uncomfortable situation—that is, if the proprietors of this stealthily acquired copyright should refuse to let me use the letters. That is what they did. (*The Autobiography of M.T.*, p. 193)

Exercise 4 State whether the underlined string of words forms a constituent.

(1) Professor Peter will meet all the students of syntax next Monday.

Exercise 5 Give a labeled bracketing representation for the following examples.

(1) The girls will buy the socks.
(2) His solution of the difficult problem will surprise all the students.

Exercise 6 Translate the following tree diagram into a labeled bracketing representation. Be careful to include only the information contained in the tree diagram.[36)]

(1)

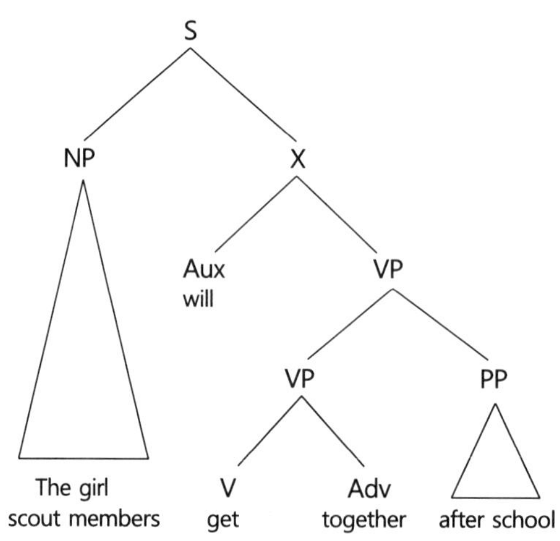

36) Triangles denote that the phrases represented by means of them are not analyzed in detail.

Exercise 7 Identify as many constituents as possible in the *students* sentence by applying the movability test to it.

(1) These students of history will be visiting the museum on Tuesday.

In addition, underline strings of words that can be argued to form constituents in the following attested data, collected by Haegeman (2006), in the light of the movability test.

(2) It's unbelievable how unlucky he's been, but he's certainly proved he's got tenacity. Whether he'll get out of this difficult situation or not, only time will tell. (*Guardian*, Feb. 8, 2003)

(3) Everything I did right for 20 years, he burned up in two or three. (*Washington Post*, Apr. 29, 2003)

Exercise 8 What do the following attested data show as regards constituency tests?

(1) Gas prices are expected to peak in Spring. What do we do now? —Mobilize and get Obama out of the White House! (sodahead.com)

(2) Not all lexemes show inflectional variation of this kind. For those that don't, the distinction between word and lexeme is unimportant. (Huddleston and Pullum 2002:16)

Exercise 9 Are the underlined strings of words constituents? For each string, provide at least one piece of evidence for your answer.

(1) Have you listened to the singer's songs?
(2) My neighbor's dog has been lost.
(3) These newly transferred students of English are participating in the Oregon Shakespeare Festival and those are going to visit London.

Exercise 10 Underline strings of words forming constituents by using the coordination test.

(1) High blood pressure may lead to brain injury and to premature brain aging, even among people with only slightly elevated readings. (*Time*, Nov. 2, 2012)

(2) The councilwoman and her family had evacuated to friends in Manasquan, about 8 km north, and were unable to return until last Wednesday. (*Time*, Nov. 5, 2012)

(3) There were no deaths or injuries reported in town, and most residents heeded the mandatory evacuation notice, ... (*Time*, Nov. 5, 2012)

Exercise 11 Each of the following quotes contains some clue(s) to claiming that a certain string of words in it forms a constituent. Underline the string of words and explain on what basis you judge that it comprises a constituent.

(1) In this book we are going to posit many hypotheses. Some of these we'll keep, others we'll revise, and still others we'll reject. (Carnie 2013:29)

(2) ... for it was by that verdict that all the lyceums in the country determined the lecture's commercial value. (*The Autobiography of Mark Twain*, pp. 217-8)

(3) Then he frankly threw himself and the house upon my mercy and begged me to take away *The Innocents Abroad* and release the concern from the contract. I said I wouldn't—and so ... (*The Autobiography of Mark Twain*, p. 208)

(4) I am sure I should have stood my ground and gone on favoring them with that tale until I broke them down, ... (*ibid*., p. 191)

(5) ... then he had to give it up and he did; (*ibid*., p. 180)

(6) "What is the prize for the ten-strike?" We had to confess that we had not selected it yet. (*ibid*., p. 180)

(7) They can't get a perspective on him and it is only by a perspective that the difference between him and the rest of their limited circle can be perceived. (*ibid*., p. 181)

(8) Doctor John was very fond of animals, and particularly of dogs. (*ibid*., p. 256)

(9) If the chairman has resigned from the board (which you say he has), how come his car is still in the company car park?

(Radford 2009:61)

(10) His conclusion: “Demonizing vendors won’t speed Florida’s recovery. Letting them go about their business will.” (Sandel 2009:5)

(11) So to decide whether price-gouging laws are justified, we need to assess these competing accounts of welfare and of freedom.

(*ibid*., p. 7)

Chapter 3
The Structure of VP and X′ Syntax

3.1 A syntactic analysis of the *students* sentence: a first step

We are now in a position to discuss the *students* sentence, repeated here for ease of reference.

(1) These students of history will be visiting the museum on Tuesday.

In (1) we intuitively recognize at least three constituents: *These students of history*, *the museum*, and *on Tuesday*. On what grounds do we justify our intuitive judgments? We justify our judgments by expanding the sentence in (1) like the following.

(2) These students of history will be visiting the museum on Tuesday.
Prof. Anderson recommended that they visit it then.

In the newly added part, *they*, *it*, and *then* are pro-forms referring to the three preceding phrases, *These students of history*, *the museum*, and *on Tuesday*, respectively, which justifies our intuitive judgments.

Next, how do we analyze the part *visiting the museum on Tuesday*? Based upon the above analysis, we can separate three constituents here: *visiting*, *the museum*, and *on Tuesday*. The problem is how these three are merged or assembled at the next stage. There are three possibilities, as illustrated below.[37)]

(3) a. [visiting$_1$ the museum$_2$] on Tuesday$_3$
b. visiting$_1$ [the museum$_2$ on Tuesday$_3$]
c. [visiting$_1$ the museum$_2$ on Tuesday$_3$]

(3c) seems to be the least plausible; previously we have claimed that the simultaneous merger of three constituents (= ternary merger) is more complex than that of two constituents (= binary merger), and accordingly, all else being equal, **binary merger** is preferred to ternary merger. Let us then put aside the analysis in (3c).

Now, how can we choose between (3a) and (3b)? Note that the two analyses assign different constituency to the part in question (that is, *visiting the museum on Tuesday*). Therefore, in order to choose between the two, we need to observe the following results obtained from applying the movement test to the original sentence in (1).

(4) a. Visiting the museum these students of history will be on Tuesday.
b. *The museum on Tuesday these students of history will be visiting.
c. On Tuesday these students of history will be visiting the museum.
d. The museum, these students of history will be visiting on Tuesday.

The results of the movement test cast doubt on the analysis in (3b) (note that (4b) is ungrammatical), while they support the analysis

37) The subscript numbers are used to mark the three constituents for ease of recognition.

in (3a) (note that (4a) is grammatical).

What happens if we move the three constituents altogether?

(5) Visiting the museum on Tuesday they will be.

Surprisingly, the resultant sentence is acceptable. Moreover, the ellipsis test also seems to support the analysis in (3c), which we have left aside because of its relative complexity.

(6) John expects that these students of history will be visiting the museum on Tuesday, and I am sure that they will be ø.

Based upon the data in (5) and (6), you might conclude that both the analyses in (3a) and (3c) are correct. However, we should be more careful in drawing such a conclusion. The reason is that if the analysis in (3c) were correct, (4a) would be predicted to be ungrammatical, contrary to fact. What the sentence in (4a) shows is that of the three given constituents, the first two, namely, *visiting* and *the museum*, merge first. What then do the sentences in (5) and (6) imply? All they show is that the three constituents form a new (larger) constituent, but not that they merge simultaneously. To conclude, we reach the following analysis. (Following the general conventions in generative syntax, we use triangles to represent phrases whose structure is not yet analyzed in detail or whose internal structure is not relevant to the discussion.)

(7) a. [[visiting the museum] on Tuesday]

b.

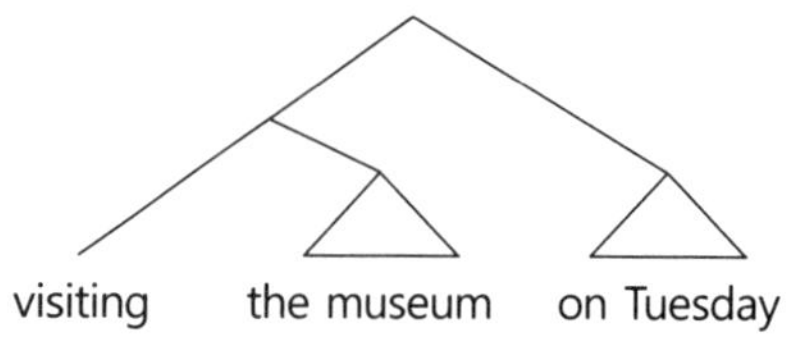

In order to recognize where we are in the analysis of the *students* sentence, let us try to represent the structure of the whole sentence. The following is the rough structural representation of the *students* sentence.

(8)

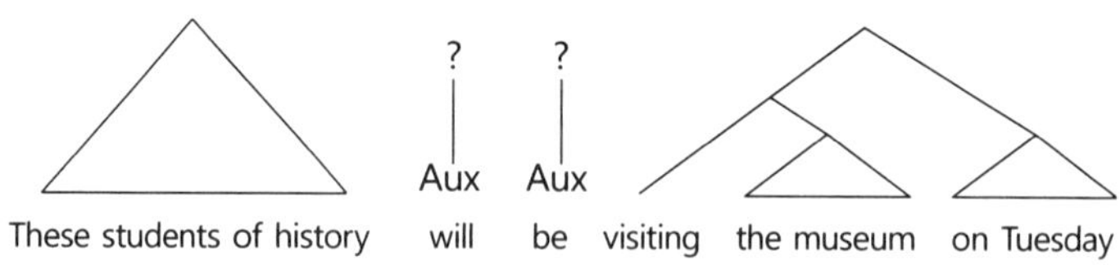

As noticeable in the above representation, if we are to describe the structure of the *students* sentence completely, we need to further analyze the structures of the three constituents, that is, the internal structures of *These students of history*, *the museum*, and *on Tuesday*. In addition, we need to clarify how the two auxiliaries *will* and *be* are merged.

3.2 Analyzing the VP structure

Before analyzing the internal structures of the three constituents mentioned in the above paragraph, let us first consider the relationships between *will*, *be*, and *visiting*. To avoid complications,[38)] let us assume that the verb *visiting* merges with the following phrases before it merges with the two preceding words, *will* and *be*. In other words, we assume that the string of words *visiting the museum on Tuesday* has formed a constituent before the merger of *visiting* with either or both of the two preceding words.[39)] Can you work out all the possible ways of merger between the three constituents, namely, *will*, *be*, *visiting ... Tuesday*? There are at least three possibilities.

(9) a.

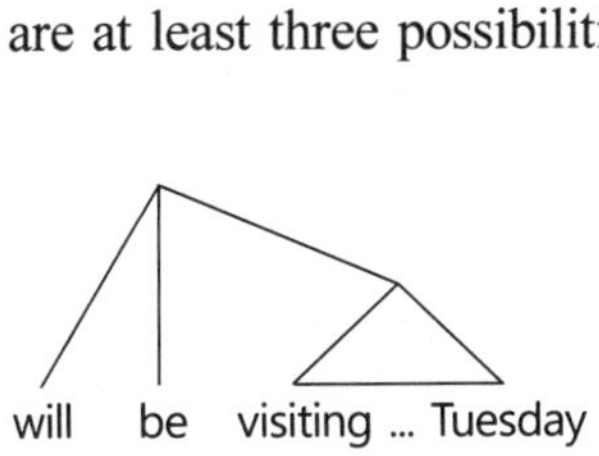

38) If our analysis is to be theoretically sound, instead of asking how the three constituents *will*, *be*, *visiting ... Tuesday* are merged, we have to address a seemingly far more difficult yet essential issue: as for the five constituents *will*, *be*, *visiting*, *the museum*, *on Tuesday*, in what order are they merged? The number of possible ways to merge five constituents is still more than that of merging three constituents. Hence, we assume that *visiting* forms a constituent with the following phrases before it merges with the preceding elements. Is this assumption of ours only for avoiding complications or is there any evidence for it? Careful readers might have already noticed that our assumption can be fully justified by the data in the text. What are they?

39) Some readers, especially those who are knowledgeable about traditional grammar, might argue against our assumption that it seems to be counter-intuitive. It is not, though. See footnote 38 and the ensuing discussion in the text.

b.

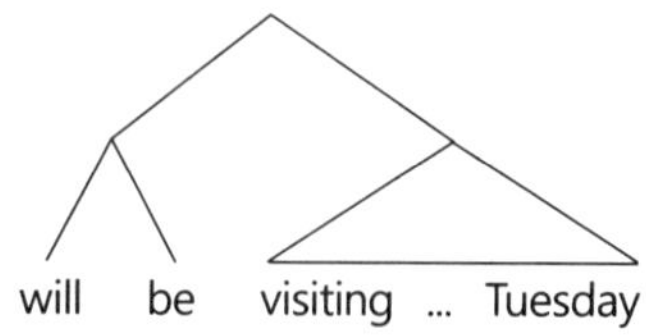

c.

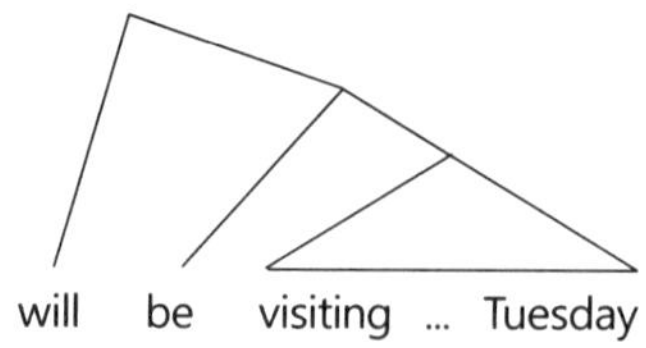

Here again, different analyses are correlated with different constituents. Thus, the analyses in (9a), (9b), and (9c) are bound up with the lists of constituents in (10a), (10b), and (10c), respectively.

(10) a. the constituents obtainable from the analysis in (9a):
will, *be*, *visiting ... Tuesday*, ***will be visiting ... Tuesday***
b. the constituents obtainable from the analysis in (9b)
will, *be*, *visiting ... Tuesday*, ***will be***, ***will be visiting ... Tuesday***
c. the constituents obtainable from the analysis in (9c)
will, *be*, *visiting ... Tuesday*, ***be visiting ... Tuesday***,
will be visiting ... Tuesday

Of these three, we will consider (9a) as the last resort, since it seems to be more complicated than the other two in the merging procedure. In order to choose between the remaining two, we need to explicate what the verb *be* merges with. If it merges with *will*, the analysis in (9b) wins out. Otherwise, the analysis in (9c) does.

Is there any supporting evidence for either of the two? Yes, there is. As can be observed in data like the following, the ellipsis test strongly supports the analysis in (9c), while it argues against that in (9b).

(11) Charles believed that these students of history will be visiting the museum on Tuesday, and I am sure that they will ø. (ø=be visiting ... Tuesday)

Note that *be visiting ... Tuesday* can wholly be elided, which proves that *be visiting ... Tuesday* is a constituent. On the other hand, if *be* formed a constituent with *will*, as asserted in the analysis in (9b), *be visiting ... Tuesday* could not form a constituent, making its ellipsis illicit, contrary to fact.

Before proceeding, it would be worthwhile to sum up the results of our analyses so far.

(12) Some principles of syntactic structure building

a. Every **word** in a sentence is the **smallest constituent** of the sentence.

b. Constituents larger than words are formed from step-by-step mergers of words, not from the simultaneous merger of all words. Thus, the structure of a sentence is not flat, but hierarchical. (**The Hierarchical Structure Principle**)

c. All the mergers of constituents up to now are binary. Thus, there seems to be no n-ary ($n \geqq 3$; ternary, tetranary, ...) merger operation in English syntax. (**The Binary Merger Principle**)

(12a) is evident from our definition of syntax: the study of how words are combined/merged into a grammatical sentence. (12b) and (12c) are generalizations gleaned from our analyses of some constituent structures so far.

At this point, it would be useful to consider what kinds of reasoning are used in scientific research, since we intend our syntactic analyses of English sentences to be scientific. In general, scientific research uses two types of reasoning: one is **inductive reasoning**, and the other **deductive reasoning.**[40)]

In leaving aside one of the three possible analyses in (9), namely, (9a), we claimed that it seems to be cognitively more complex than the other alternatives. However, we can justify our preclusion using deductive reasoning as well. Let me be more specific to help you understand. In (12) there are three generalizations stated concerning syntactic structure building in English, by definition ((12a)) or on the basis of previous analyses of some English sentences ((12b, c)). Now we can use the generalization in (12c), the so-called **Binary Merger Principle (BMP)**, in excluding (9a). According to the BMP, every merger of syntactic constituents is binary. When faced with choosing between the three possible analyses ((9a)-(9c)) of the relationship between the auxiliaries and the main verb,[41)] we can

---

40) Note the following typical examples of inductive (i) and deductive (ii) reasoning.

(i) a. Socrates died.
  b. King Sejong died.
  c. Therefore, all human beings die.
(ii) a. All human beings die.
  b. Sagang is a one-hundred-three-year-old French woman.
   (Women are human beings.)
  c. Therefore, Sagang must die after all.

41) There arises the problem of categorizing words like *will, be, have, can, may*, etc., which have been classified as auxiliaries in traditional grammar. Following traditional grammar, we will categorize them as auxiliaries, without argument. For further discussion, see chapter 4.

utilize the BMP. The reasoning is as follows: the BMP, as a sort of generalization, has been valid for analyses of other structures, and therefore we deduce that it can also be applied to analyzing the auxiliary + auxiliary + main verb sequence, without further argument. Thus, the BMP leads us to exclude ternary mergers like (9a).

3.3 The structures of other phrases

In the course of analyzing the *students* sentence, we have identified three constituents—*these students of history*, *the museum*, and *on Tuesday*—apart from the VP. Obviously, they are categorized as NP, NP, and PP, respectively. As we noted in chapter 1, we categorize a certain phrase as XP, if it contains X as the head of the phrase. Thus, the three constituents are categorized and labeled as NP, NP, and PP, since their heads are *students* (N), *museum* (N), and *on* (P), respectively. What is at issue is how to analyze the element(s) surrounding the head of a phrase and how to characterize them with respect to the head.[42] Before entering into detailed discussion, let us define the head and give some examples.

---

42) In traditional grammar elements surrounding the head of a phrase are called modifiers, which, in turn, are subclassified further. For instance, modifiers of a noun head are classified into pre-modifiers and post-modifiers. Determiners as typical pre-modifiers of nouns are again distinguished into pre-, central, and post-determiners. Note that those subclassifications consider only relataive linear order of elements.

(13) Head: when X and Y merge, X is the head of the merger if it determines the syntactic nature of the whole, it selects Y, and the result of the merger denotes a kind of X.

(14) Examples

a. *tall boys*: head = *boys*

① Syntactically, *tall boys* behaves like a noun, not an adjective.
(i) John looks {happy/*tall boys}; {John/Tall boys} danced.

② *Tall boys* denotes a kind of 'boys,' not a kind of 'tallness.'

b. *meet* + *tall boys*: head = *meet*

① Syntactically, *meet tall boys* behaves like a verb, not a noun.
(i) {John/*Meet tall boys} looks happy; John {ran/met tall boys}.

② *Meet* selects *tall boys* as its object, requiring the accusative case if the latter is a pronoun (*meet* {**they*/**their*/*them*}).

③ *Meet tall boys* denotes a kind of 'meeting,' not a kind of 'boys.'

Knowing what the head of a phrase is is essential for determining the label/category of the phrase concerned. Let us now analyze the internal structure of each constituent of the *students* sentence.

3.3.1 The NP structure

With the characteristic properties of a head in mind, let us try to analyze the structure of the first phrasal constituent, repeated below.

(15) these students of history

In light of the defining properties of a head, summarized in (13), the head of the phrase in (15) is *students,*[43] which leads us to categorize the whole phrase as NP. Now how do we analyze its internal structure? In theory, the NP can be analyzed in one of the following three ways.[44]

(16) a.

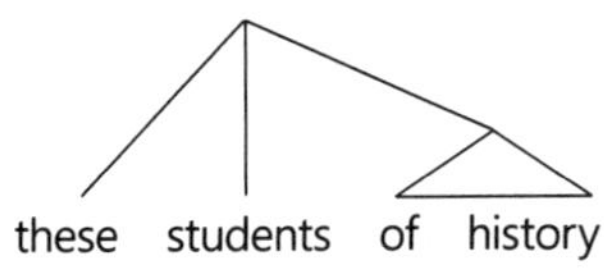

b.

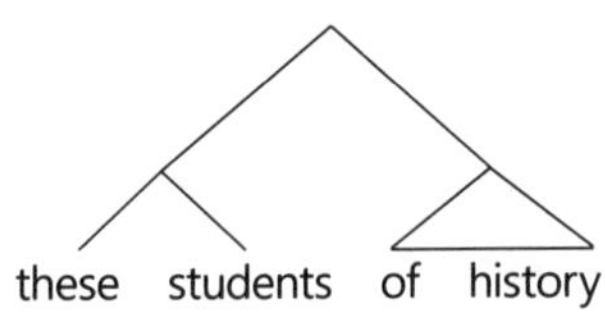

c.

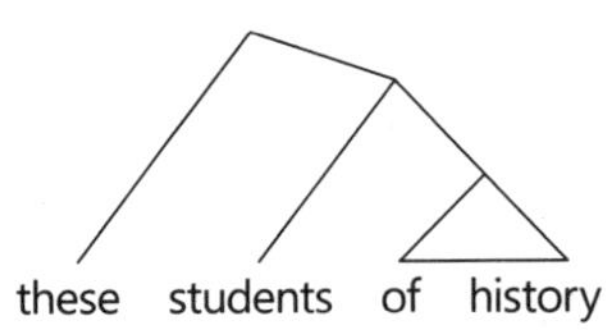

If we assume that every phrase necessarily has a head[45] and is built up through only step-by-step binary mergers, (16a) is ruled

---

43) How can you justify this statement?

44) We assume here that *of* and *history* form a constituent of their own before merging with *these* and *students*. Otherwise, there would be far more possible ways of analysis. How can you justify the assumption?

45) All generative syntacticians take this for granted and seems to adopt the following principle.

(i) **The Headedness Principle**
Every constituent must be headed, i.e., must have a head.
(cf. Radford 2004:61, 341; Carnie 2013:173))

out due to the BMP. Consequently, we have to choose between (16b) and (16c). Which do you think is the correct analysis and why? Observe the following examples that seem relevant to your decision.

(17) These students of history will visit the museum, but those ø won't. (ø= students of history)

(18) These students of history are from Germany, while those ø are from Italy. (ø= students of history)

The data in (17)-(18) show that *students of history* can be deleted, hence it is evident that *students* and *of history* form a constituent. On the other hand, the following data show that *These students* cannot be a constituent. Note that it is irreplaceable by *they*.

(19) These students are studying harder than they did last semester. (they = these students)

(20) These students of history will visit the British Museum, and *they of physics will visit the Leaning Tower of Pisa. (they = these students)

Based upon the above arguments, we are led to adopt the analysis in (16c).

The next issue that we face is how to differentiate the two non-head elements of the NP, i.e., *these* and *of history*. As can be noticed in the tree diagram in (16c), the head *students* is more closely related to *of history* than to *these*.[46] In this connection,

46) It should be borne in mind that if X (= head) and Y are first merged and then Z

it would be helpful to note the parallel relationship that can be observed in the following pair.

(21) a. these students of history
b. these people who study history

More specifically, the (semantic) relationship between *students* and *of history* shows a close parallel to that between *study* and *history*. Thus, we may say that just as *history* is the object of the verb *study*, so the phrase *of history* can be said to function as the "semantic" object of the noun *students*. To capture this functional similarity of *history* and *of history*, Chomsky suggests that the two phrases be dubbed the "complement" of their head. That is to say, *of history* is the complement of the head *students*, and *history* is the complement of the head *study*.

What about the remaining part, that is, the pre-modifier *these*? While the referential domain of *students of history* is rather vague, that of *these students of history* seems to be more specified due to the determiner *these*. As a consequence we can say that *these* plays the role of specifying the reference of the head noun *students*. Hence we dub *these* "specifier." The discussion so far leads to the following analysis.

---

is merged with the result of the first merger, it implies that X is syntactically and semantically closer to Y than to Z.

(22)[47]

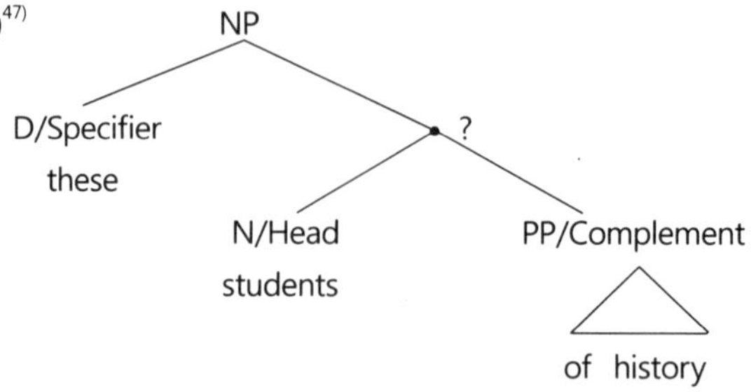

The tree diagram in (22) contains the following information. The noun phrase *these students of history* consists of three constituents. Of the three, the noun *students* is the head of the phrase, takes the PP *of history* as its complement and first merges with the latter. Then, the resulting category corresponding to ? merges with the determiner *these*, which plays the role of the specifier of NP (or N).

At this stage of analysis there emerge two questions. First, what label is assigned to the ?-marked node? Second, how can we justify our categorization of *of history* as a PP? For the time being, let us set aside the second problem and try to solve the first question. A careful observation of the above tree diagram would reveal that the head N gets bigger and bigger by merging with its neighboring elements. We call this process the "**projection**" of N. In more detail, the head noun first merges with its complement and **projects** into a larger nominal constituent, marked with ? in (22), and the newly formed nominal constituent, in turn, merges with

47) Note that N, D, and PP are categorial labels, whereas head, complement, and specifier are functional labels. In other words, N, D, and PP denote the category of a word or phrase, while the terms head, complement, and specifier denote the function of a word or phrase with respect to its neighboring word or phrase.

the specifier, projecting into NP.

Here we need to differentiate the three levels of nominal projection: the head level (N), the intermediate level (?) between N and NP, and the maximal level (NP). Notice that we have labels for the head level and the maximal level, namely, N and NP, respectively. Can't we invent a label to refer to the intermediate level for short? With respect to this problem we are indebted to Chomsky, who suggests the label N′.[48] If we now describe the tree diagram in (22) using the new terms, N projects into N′(read as "n-bar") by merging with its complement, and N′ in turn projects into N″(= NP; read as "n-double-bar") by merging with the specifier. The three-step projection[49] of N can be illustrated by the following examples of NPs.

(23) a. [$_{N''(=NP)}$ John's [$_{N'}$ [$_{N}$ **construction**] of the bridge]]]
b. [$_{N''(=NP)}$ a criminal's [$_{N'}$ [$_{N}$ **assassination**] of J. F. Kennedy]]]
c. [$_{N''(=NP)}$ the [$_{N'}$ [$_{N}$ **revival**] of Korean traditional music]]]

It should be remembered, however, that not every NP contains both a complement and a specifier. For instance, *John*, *the book*, and *students of English,* despite their lack of a complement and/or a specifier, must be all treated as NPs, not as N or N′. Their status as an NP is well-grounded because they can occur in the typical

48) The term N-bar originates in Chomsky's (1970) use of $\bar{N}$ as the relevant notation. Later, the notation has been changed to the current form N′, perhaps for typographical convenience.

49) The three-level projections are often distinguished as "minimal projection" (= the head N^0), "intermediate projection" (= N′), and "maximal projection" (= N″ or NP) (see Chomsky 1995). Throughout this book, we will use only N′. In the case of N^0 and N″, we will continue to use the corresponding traditional labels N and NP instead.

NP positions of a sentence, as exemplified below.

(24) {John/The book/Her love for him} is easy to understand.

Based upon the above discussion we may propose a general skeletal structure for analyzing/generating NPs as follows.[50)]

(25)

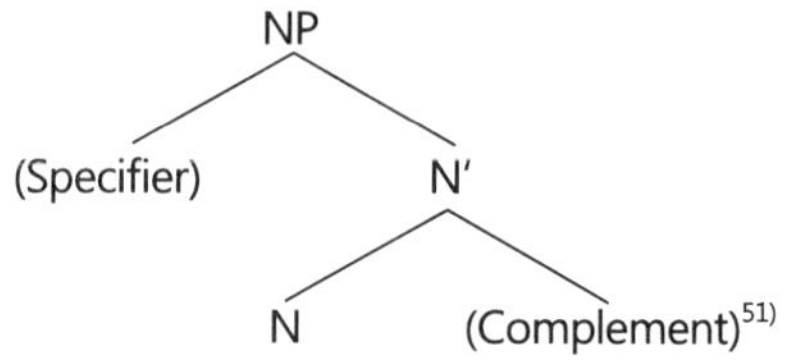

At this point let us attempt to define the specifier and the complement, as we did with regard to the head. Roughly, we can define the complement as the element that a head requires semantically. For example, the transitive verb *study* requires an object of study for the completion of its meaning, and it is quite natural to refer to the verb's object as its "complement." The same is true of the PPs contained in (23a-c), which seem to complete the nominal heads in bold type. Thus, we can provide the following definition of complement.

(26) X is a complement of Y if X is required for the (semantic) completion of Y.

50) Analyzing reflects the viewpoint of the hearer/grammarians, while generating reflects the viewpoint of the speaker.

51) As is customary in linguistics, we use parentheses to indicate the optionality of an element. Hereafter, however, let us omit parentheses in a tree.

Next, how do we define the specifier? In the case of (21a), the determiner *these* seems to specify the referential domain of *students of history*, hence justifying the term "specifier." However, this characterization is likely to face difficulty in accounting for the specifiers in (23a, b). One might insist that they also specify the referential domain of the following nominal expressions, but no one can deny that the specifiers are also the semantic "subject" of the head noun. This is evident from the fact that (23a, b) express basically the same meaning as their corresponding sentences given below.

(27) a. John constructed the bridge.
b. A criminal assassinated J. F. Kennedy.

Another striking similarity between the subject of a sentence and the specifier of an NP is that both can show number agreement. Observe the following data.

(28) a. The student {*study/studies} hard.
b. The students {study/*studies} hard.

(29) a. I met {this/*these} student at the market.
b. {*This/These} new discoveries led to a scientific revolution.

As a fourth characteristic property of the specifier we can point out its linear order with respect to the head: the specifier always precedes the head.

All in all, the specifier can be characterized as follows.

(30) Properties of the specifier
  a. The specifier specifies the referential domain of the head.
  b. The specifier can be the semantic subject of the head.
  c. The specifier can show number agreement with the head.
  d. The specifier always precedes the head.

The above discussion brings forth the following analyses of the NPs in (21a) and (23).

(31)

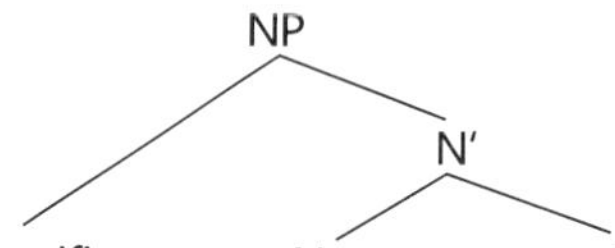

Specifier	N	Complement
these	students	of history
John's	construction	of the bridge
a criminal's	assassination	of J. F. Kennedy
the	revival	of Korean traditional music

3.3.2 The PP structure

Let us now turn to the second problem, which relates to prepositional phrases (PP). First, observe some examples of PPs, including the phrase *of history*, which is included in the *students* sentence.

(32) a. of history
  b. between the two lovers
  c. right across the street
  d. straight up the tree

Like transitive verbs, prepositions usually cannot be used alone, requiring an NP. As a concrete example, *between the two lovers* is formed by merging the preposition *between* and the NP *the two lovers*. Why do we label the whole phrase as PP rather than as NP? The reason is that *between* is the head of the whole phrase. The assigning of the head status to *between* is attributed to at least two factors. First, in merging the two elements, *between* and *the two lovers,* the former requires the latter, while the latter can stand on its own as an NP. Second, *between* selects *the two lovers,* determining its case form. Thus, *between them* is correct, but not **between {they/their}*. As a natural consequence of assigning the head status to *between*, *the two lovers* takes the role of complement.

In like manner, the phrases in (32a, c, d) are also analyzed as PPs. An additional issue that is raised about (32c, d) is how to treat the words *right* and *straight* in front of the head. From a semantic viewpoint, they seem to specify the locational domain denoted by the following expression, e.g. *across the street*. In addition, they always precede the head. (Recall at this point that the specifier always precedes the head in other phrases!) Consequently, we analyze the two words as specifiers. To sum up, we arrive at the following structural analysis of PPs.

(33)

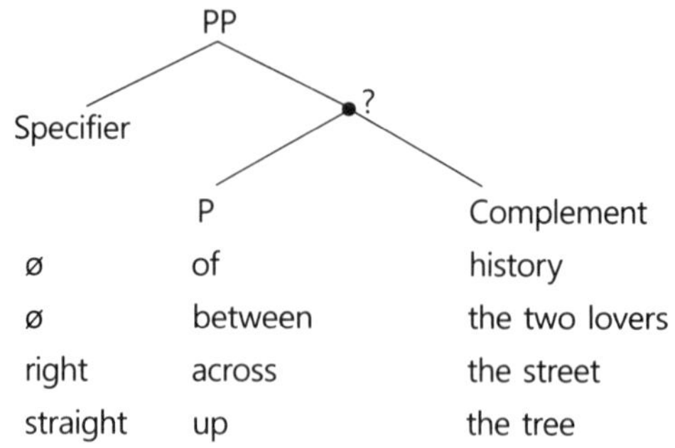

The residual issue is: what label do we assign to the ?-marked node? Needless to say, labeling it P′ would be appropriate, since by doing so, we can unify the NP and PP structures into a generalized structural format using the variable X, as displayed below.

(34)

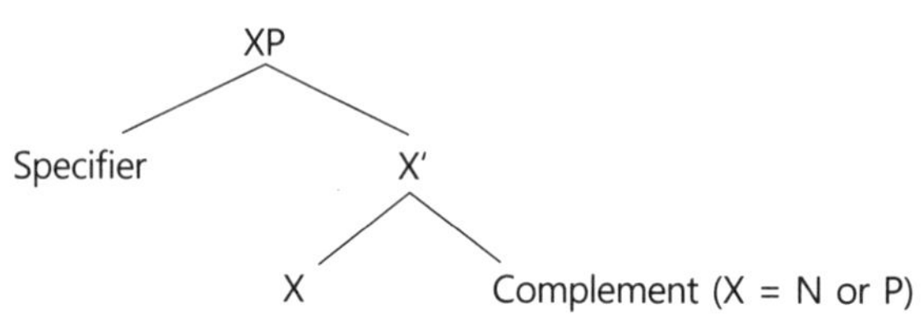

Now that we analyzed NPs and PPs, let us turn to the problem of analyzing the *students* sentence as a whole. Fortunately, we have already explicated the (structural) relationship between the auxiliary and the main verb.[52] The analyses so far enable us to draw the following tree diagram for the *students* sentence.

---

52) In order to avoid complications in argumentation, let us leave out one of the two auxiliaries and deal with this simplified sentence: *These students of history will visit the museum on Tuesday.*

(35)

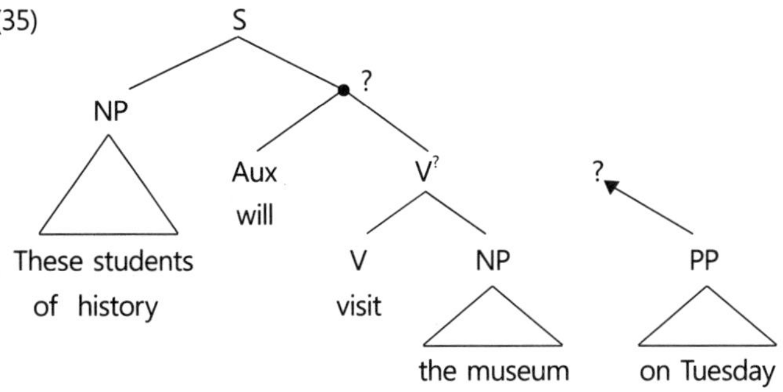

At a glance we notice that we are still far away from our goal—the complete analysis of the whole sentence. To attain our goal we have to answer at least three questions. First, when the auxiliary *will* and $V^?$ merge, which is the head? Second, what is the level of $V^?$? Is it V′ or VP? The answer to the second question is likely to hinge on that to the first question. Third, where is the sentence-final PP—*on Tuesday*—attached? Let us deal with these questions in turn.

When *will* and *visit the museum* merge, which do you think is the head of the merger? In the light of the general characteristics of a head, *will* must be the head. First, while *visit the museum* is complete as a linguistic expression without any auxiliary, the auxiliary *will* cannot stand alone without a main verb (+complement). Second, *will* selects the following verb and determines its form, as exemplified by *I will {visit/*visits/*visiting/*visited} him tomorrow*.

Building upon the answer to the first question, we are now in a position to answer the second question: is $V^?$ V′ or VP? Being a head, *will* cannot be the specifier of the main verb. Rather, the following phrase *visit the museum* is the complement of *will*. Consequently, $V^?$ has to be VP.

At this point, some might be satisfied with our solutions, since we seem to have resolved the two problems almost at the same time, but we face a new question: what label do we assign to the ?-marked node? Is it Aux′ or AuxP? For the moment, let us assume that it is an AuxP.[53)] How then do we analyze the relationship between the subject and the AuxP? More specifically, when the subject NP and the AuxP merge, which is the head? Traditional grammarians thought that the merger of the subject and the predicate (=AuxP in our terms) resulted in a completely new category,[54)] that is, a S(entence), not a phrase. Thus, the category S(entence) is distinctly differentiated from both words and phrases. This analysis implies that neither the subject NP nor the AuxP is the head of the merger.

From a scientific perspective, this state of affairs is quite undesirable. As was indicated previously, linguistic expressions are generated by merging only two constituents at a time. (Recall the BMP!) In addition, every merger selects one of the two as the head of the resulting expression, in accordance with the **Headedness Principle** (see footnote 45). Now if the merger of the subject NP and the AuxP results in an S, a headless expression, this is exceptional and idiosyncratic. If the sentence is truly exceptional,

53) As of now we cannot but accept this assumption if we take the tree diagram in (35) to be correct. In other words, if we assume that the ?-marked node is Aux′, the higher node S should be changed to AuxP. Pay attention to the ensuing discussion in the text.

54) Here "completely new" means 'having nothing to do with the two merging elements.'

as asserted by traditional grammarians, we must explain why. By contrast, if we could eliminate the exceptional property of the S category, the syntactic structural system would be simpler and more elegant.

Confronted with this troublesome situation, we need to carefully examine our assumption that the ?-marked node is labeled AuxP. What if we assume that the label is Aux′ instead? If the merger of the auxiliary and the VP is taken to result in Aux′ in accordance with our new assumption, there emerges the possibility of reanalyzing the sentence level as AuxP. In other words, on the proposed reanalysis, we need not use the exceptional S label at all!

However, the reanalysis necessitates an additional assumption: the subject NP is the specifier of the AuxP. Can we justify this additional assumption? Sure we can! Recall that one of the characteristics of the specifier is that it can show agreement with the head. Although modal auxiliaries might not appear to show agreement superficially, in fact, they do. This can be easily seen if we change the modal auxiliary to the perfect auxiliary.

(36) a. These students of history {*has/have} visited the British Museum three times.
b. This student of history {has/*have} visited the British Museum three times.

Thus, we have a good reason to regard the subject as the specifier of the AuxP.

On our new analysis, the traditional level of sentence is reduced to a sort of phrase, not unlike other phrases. More specifically, the sentence is merely an AuxP. Now if we adopt the new analysis, we obtain the following tree diagram for the *students* sentence.

(37)

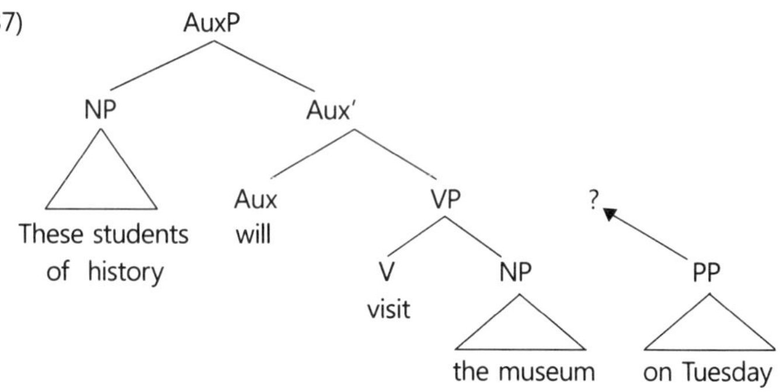

While it is true that the tree diagram in (37) tells us many new things about the structure of the *students* sentence, it also raises some additional questions. Above all else, where does the PP *on Tuesday* attach? It must be contained in the VP in view of the following data.

(38) The chair of the department expects that these students of history will visit the museum on Tuesday, and visit the museum on Tuesday they will.

But it is not clear how it is merged with the other constituents in the VP, namely, the verb *visit* and its complement *the museum*. The BMP prevents it from being merged with the two constituents simultaneously. (Note that the presumed merger produces a ternary-branching structure against the BMP.)

As pointed out earlier, if a head takes both a complement and a specifier, the head first merges with the complement and then the resulting expression merges with the specifier. This order of merger is not arbitrary. Rather, it reflects the fact that the semantic relationship between the head and the complement is closer than that between the head and the specifier. Now, what about the semantic relationships between the head verb *visit* and the two constituents, *the museum* and *on Tuesday*? The relationship between *visit* and *the museum* is claimed to be closer than that between *visit* and *on Tuesday*, for two reasons. First, *the museum* cannot be omitted without making the VP ungrammatical, while *on Tuesday* can, as shown below.

(39) a. *They will visit on Tuesday.
   b. They will visit the museum.

Thus, syntacticians distinguish the two constituents by naming them complement and adjunct, respectively. Second, the linear order of the two constituents cannot be changed without making the VP ungrammatical.

(40) a. *They will visit on Tuesday the museum.
   b. *They will on Tuesday visit the museum.

Some might suggest that we treat the PP as the specifier of VP. We cannot do so, however, because, as evidenced in (40b), the PP cannot precede the head (= *visit*), which is generally required of a specifier in English.

It is clear from the discussion that the adjunct must be attached to V′ or VP. Unfortunately, syntacticians are divided in their opinion about this problem. Some claim that it must be attached to V′ and others assert that it must be attached to VP. And there are still others who concede that the adjunct can be attached in either position. Let us assume without further argument that the third position is correct. Thus, we arrive at the following structural analysis.

(41)

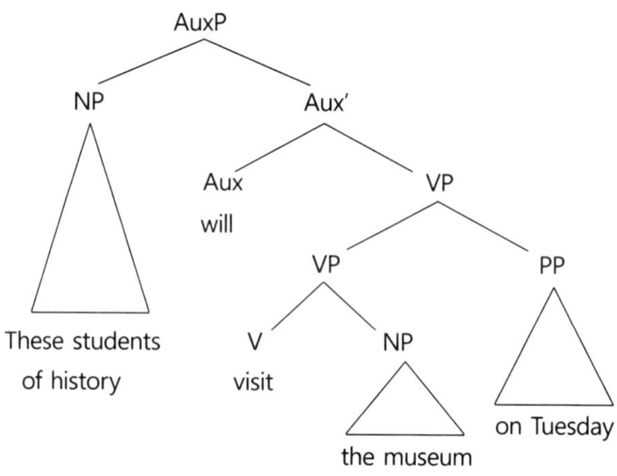

Is this then the complete picture of the structure of the *students* sentence? It might seem to be, but a careful reader might be curious about this: why does the VP lack the specifier position, unlike other phrases such as NP, PP, and AuxP? Is it an accidental gap or is there anything wrong with our analysis? In the next chapter we will deal with this problem.

3.4 Linguistic generalization: X′ syntax

Before concluding the present chapter, we will do two things. One is to show how we can achieve simplicity through generalization in a scientific study of English syntax. The other is to introduce some terminology for facilitating discussion based upon tree diagrams. This section is devoted to the former. For discussion, let us observe the following data, paying special attention to the internal structure of the underlined parts.

(42) a. Bell's invention of the telephone was revolutionary. NP
b. John will *notice the bulletin*. AuxP (***VP***)
c. Anne was very fond of dogs. AP
d. The post office is right across the street. PP
e. Leibniz investigated calculus quite independently of Newton. AdvP

If we analyze the underlined parts one after another, we obtain the following tree diagrams as a result:[55)]

55) All the underlined parts in (42a, c-e) must arguably be maximal projections if we accept that only maximal projections (i.e., XP, but not X or X′) can be moved, as claimed by Radford (2009). Observe the following data.

(i) a. She certainly seems to be very proud of him.
b. Very proud of him, she certainly seems to be.
c. *Proud of him, she certainly seems to be very. (Radford 2009:55)

(ii) a. She hit him right on the nose.
b. Right on the nose, she hit him.
c. *On the nose, she hit him right. (Radford 2009:54)

If we apply movement to the underlined parts in (41a, c-e), we obtain the same results, which testifies that they are all maximal projections.

(43) a.

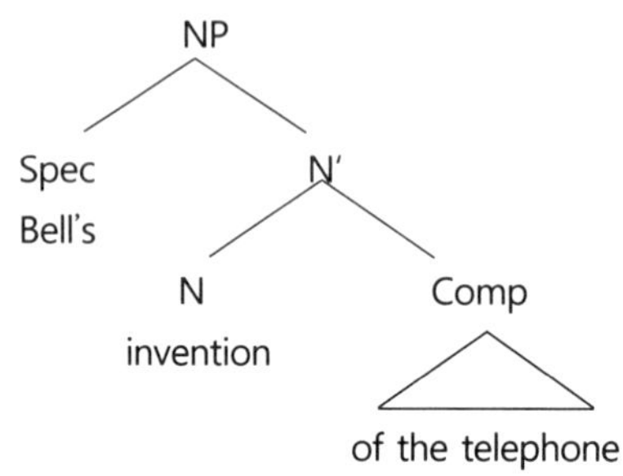
NP
Spec
Bell's
N'
N
invention
Comp
of the telephone

b.

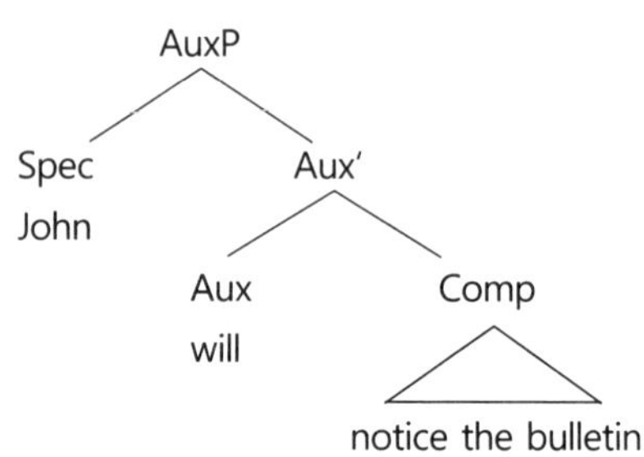
AuxP
Spec
John
Aux'
Aux
will
Comp
notice the bulletin

c.

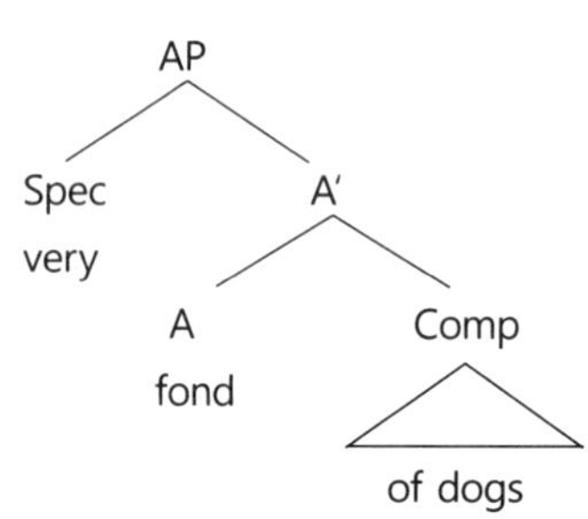
AP
Spec
very
A'
A
fond
Comp
of dogs

d.

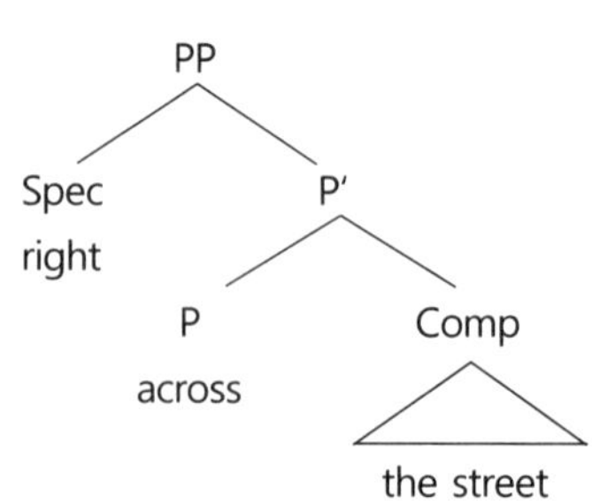
PP
Spec
right
P'
P
across
Comp
the street

e.

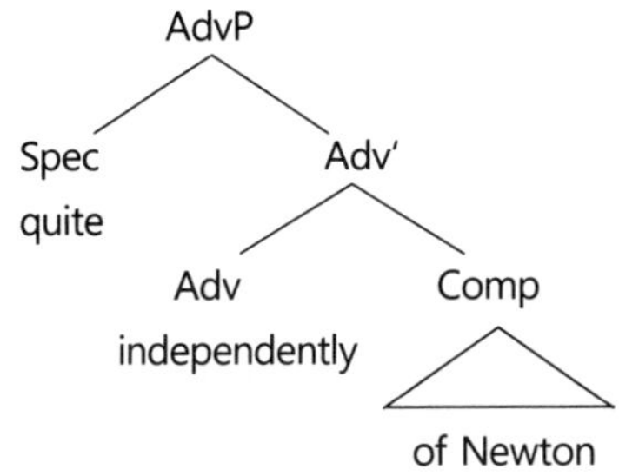

The five tree diagrams can be considered to be different from each other since obviously the categories of their heads are different from one another. On the other hand, if we lay focus on the way each head is projected into its maximal projection, we notice that all the phrases show quite the same steps of projection: the head merges with the complement, projecting into its intermediate projection, which in turn merges with the specifier, projecting into the maximal projection. Now how can we capture this commonality? We can do so by creating a variable X and making it have N, Aux, A, P, or Adv as its value. This means that all the syntactic structures in (43) can be subsumed by the following tree diagram containing the head X.

(44)

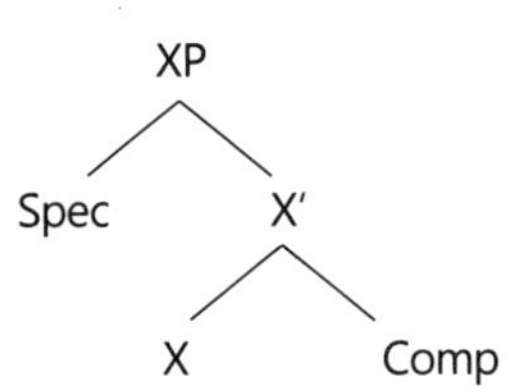

(X=N, Aux, A, P, or Adv)

The process of generalization introduced above might seem to be a funny trick, but in fact, its implications are very important indeed. If we finish analyzing the structures of the underlined parts in (42) by providing the tree diagrams in (43), we are likely to imply that in English there are five separate trees for forming phrases. By contrast, if we unify them into the abstract structure in (44), it implies that the five sorts of phrases are formed by a single tree, namely, the tree in (44). In other words, syntactic trees for forming phrases in English are simplified as one.

To help understand significance of generalization, it would be helpful to exemplify mathematical generalization. Observe the following sequence of numbers.

(45) 4, 5, 7, 10, 14, 19, 25, ...

How do we characterize the sequence in (45)? There are two ways to do it.

(46) a. The first term is 4. The other terms are determined such that the n-th term is obtained by adding n-1 to the (n-1)th term.
b. The n-th term of the sequence is determined by the following formula.

$$a_n = 4 + \frac{n^2 - n}{2} \quad (a_n = \text{n-th term})$$

At a glance the two characterizations might seem to be identical, because they produce the same result. However, they are very different in predictive power. For instance, how do you know the 100th term of the series? If you adopt the characterization in (46a), you have to know the 99th term, which will require you to obtain the 98th term, ... That is, if you want to know the 100th term, you have to know all the numbers in the series from the first to the 99th term. On the other hand, with the generalized formula in (46b), you can get the 100th term by simply substituting 100 for n in it. Which has greater predictive power and is more efficient? Needless to say, it is the characterization in (46b).

One of Chomsky's ingenious contributions to linguistics is that he has attempted to apply mathematical or more broadly scientific methodology to the study of language. The unification of the trees for forming phrases into one by means of the variable X is an example of his ingenuity.

Here let us introduce another method for capturing the information contained in the tree in (44). The tree in (44) provides us with at least two pieces of information: ① the maximal projection XP is composed of X′ plus the specifier; ② the intermediate projection X′ is composed of the head X plus the complement. These two facts can be captured by the combination of the following two rules (for detailed illustration of this kind of rules, see Chomsky 1957, 1965, among others).

(47) a. XP → Specifier + X′ (→ reads "rewrites as," or "consists of.")
b. X′ → X + Complement

These rules generate the tree in (44) if both of them are applied in turn. Moreover, if we posit that the variable can have any of the five categories as its value, those rules can generate all kinds of phrase structures. Hence, they are called **phrase structure rules**. Since Chomsky (1970), these generalized rules for forming phrases and the corresponding skeletal tree format have been considered to constitute **X′ syntax/theory**.

Viewed from the perspective of X′ theory, the VP structure is exceptional in that it does not seem to have a specifier position and therefore cannot be subsumed under the theory. In retrospect, we were in a very similar situation in analyzing the sentence level. As was pointed out in the foregoing, the traditional analysis of the sentence level made it impossible to unify it with the analysis of phrases, since unlike phrases, the sentence has traditionally been considered to be non-headed. We have resolved this exceptionality of the sentence level by showing that the sentence can be reanalyzed as an AuxP. Why then don't we attempt to reanalyze the VP so that it can be subsumed by the general skeletal X′ structure for phrases? If the VP could be analyzed to fit into X′ syntax, we would be able to say that all phrases, needless to say, including the sentence level, can be analyzed by means of the phrase structure rules and general skeletal tree structure provided by X′ theory.

(48) X′ theory
 a. Phrase structure rules
  (i) XP → Specifier + X′ (Specifier Rule)
  (ii) X′ → X + Complement (Complement Rule)
  (iii) a. X′ → Adjunct + X′ (Adjunct Rules)
   b. XP → XP + Adjunct

b. Skeletal tree structure[56]

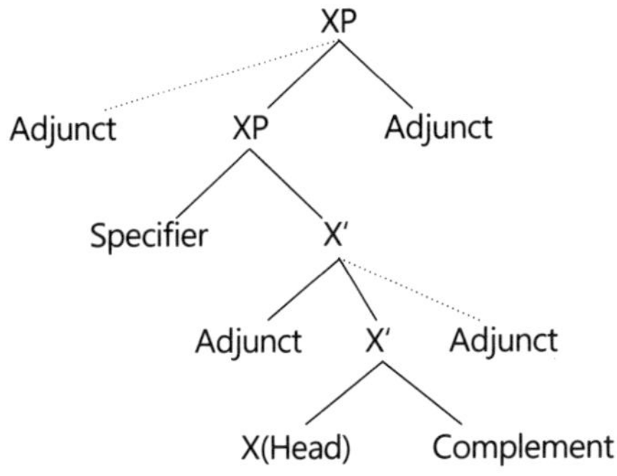

For now, we have no motivation for claiming that the VP should be analyzed in accordance with the general X′ theory, except that such an analysis would allow us to subsume all phrases under a common structural analysis. In other words, it would be theoretically desirable if we could unify the analysis of VP with that of other phrases. However, in order to claim that kind

56) The skeletal structure in (48b) is more complicated than that in (44) due to the inclusion of adjuncts. Note that locations for adjuncts are more flexible, compared with those for the specifier and complement. Thus, specifiers are always placed before their heads, and complements follow their heads, but adjuncts can be placed in either side of their sisters, as indicated by the dotted lines in (48b). Observe the following tree diagram instantiating the skeletal structure in (48b).

(i)

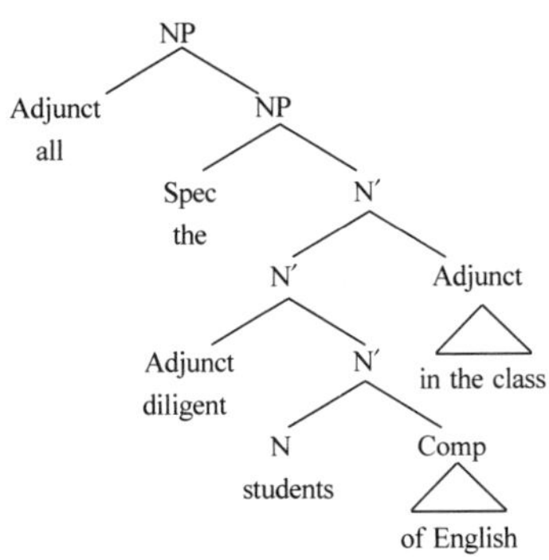

of analysis is correct, we need to find some empirical evidence for postulating the specifier position of VP. In later chapters we will provide some empirical as well as conceptual evidence for claiming that the VP can be analyzed in conformity with X′ theory like other phrases.

3.5 Terminology for tree diagrams

According to our analysis, the sentence is a special sort of *phrase*, namely, AuxP, and we do not need to use the category S/Clause any more. Consequently, in analyzing sentence structures, we have only to investigate how "phrases" are formed. As repeatedly pointed out previously, phrases (now including AuxPs, which are identified with sentences) are formed by a series of binary merger operations. In addition, the resulting structures can be represented by means of tree diagrams. Tree diagrams are also called phrase-markers since they mark how words are merged together to form various types of phrases. By providing tree diagrams for sentences, we can demonstrate their structural information.

In order to facilitate our discussion concerning structural relations between syntactic constituents of a sentence, based upon its tree diagram, we need to get acquainted with some terminology for tree diagrams. For a concrete illustration, let us take a look at the following abstract tree diagram, and try to get used to the relevant terms.

(49)

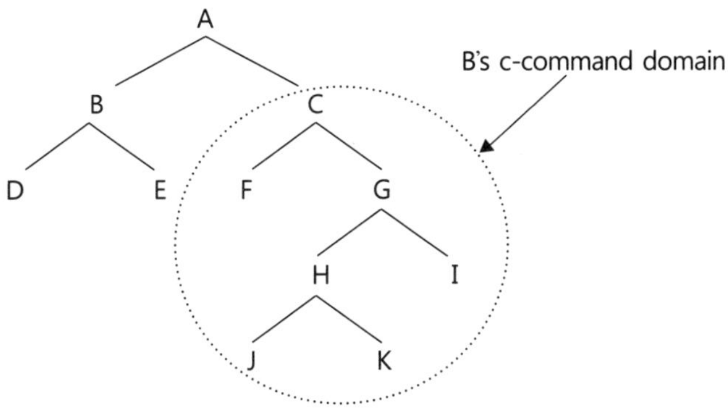

a. A, B, C, ... K are all category labels. The points at which those category labels are assigned are called **nodes.**
   ① The topmost node A is called the **root node.**
   ② A node from which no downward line is drawn is called a terminal node. The nodes D, E, F, J, K, and I are **terminal nodes.** Every terminal node hosts a **lexical item** (=word) selected from the lexicon (=mental dictionary).
   ③ Nodes other than terminal ones are called **non-terminal nodes.** A, B, C, G, and H are **non-terminal nodes.**

b. If a node is higher than another in the tree and one or more downward lines link the two, the former is said to **dominate** the latter. In the above tree, A **dominates** all the other nodes, while C dominates F, G, H, I, J, and K.[57] If a node dominates another and they are linked with one line, we say that the former **immediately dominates** the latter. For instance, A immediately dominates B and C, and G immediately dominates H and I.

c. The lines connecting two nodes are called **branches.** We may notice from the tree that all the non-terminal nodes are **binary-branching;** there is no ternary- or tetranary-branching node.

57) Of course, B cannot dominate any of the set {F, G, H, I, J, K}, although it is located in a higher position than the set members. Note that in order to connect B and any one of the latter, an upward line is needed.

d. In addition to the terms **dominate/immediately dominate**, syntacticians use terms borrowed from words denoting family relationships. Thus, if a node immediately dominates another, the former is the **mother** of the latter, while the latter is a **daughter** of the former. For example, A is the **mother** of B and C, while B and C are the **daughters** of A. If two or more nodes share a node as their mother node, the former are **sisters** to each other. According to this definition, B and C are **sisters.**

e. The most interesting and useful term for tree diagrams is **c-command.** C-command is defined as: **a node X** is taken to **c-command** its **sister** and **all the nodes dominated by the latter.** For instance, B c-commands all the nodes contained in the dotted circle in (49). They altogether constitute the **c-command domain** of B.[58)]

What should be noticed concerning tree diagrams like the one above is that they have a hierarchical structure, not a flat one. If the sentence had a flat structure, syntactic phenomena in a sentence would be accounted for by considering the linear word order alone. On the other hand, if the sentence has a hierarchical structure, as shown and reflected in the above tree diagram, we may well expect there to be some syntactic phenomena for whose explication the hierarchical relations between constituents play a crucial role.

The following two sets of data support the hierarchical analysis rather than the flat one. Observe the first set below.[59)]

(50) a. <u>Columbus</u> expected that <u>he</u> would discover America.

---

58) The concept of c-command was proposed by Reinhart (1976, 1983).

59) In each sentence, the underlined words are considered to refer to the same person, that is, to be coreferential.

b. *He expected that Columbus would discover America.
c. If people had not believed that he would discover America, Columbus would not have left his hometown.
d. If people had not expected that Columbus would discover America, he would not have left his hometown.

We usually define pronouns as words referring to some *preceding* nouns. Such a definition considers only the relative linear order of nouns and their coreferential pronouns. With that definition, however, we cannot account for all the uses of pronouns observed in the above data. More specifically, if we adopt the above definition of pronouns, we can predict the (un) grammaticality of the examples in (50a, b, d). However, how can we explain the grammaticality of (50c) by means of the definition, which takes into account only the linear order of nouns and their corresponding pronouns?

On the other hand, if we postulate the following constraint on the use of pronouns on the basis of the hierarchical relations between pronouns and their **antecedents**,[60)] we can explain away the above data.

(51) **Pronouns cannot c-command their antecedents.**

The sentence in (50b) is ungrammatical because the subject pronoun c-commands its antecedent contained in the subordinate clause. In the other examples, the pronoun *he* cannot be considered

60) Modern syntacticians use the term "antecedent" to refer to the noun with which a pronoun is coreferential.

to c-command its antecedent, which explains their grammaticality. (Note that the subject *he* c-commands only the predicate part of its own clause, that is, *would discover America/would not have left his hometown.*)[61]

Let us discuss the second set of data due to Radford.

(52) a. **Nobody** will complain about anything.
 b. **If** anyone should ask for me, say I've gone to lunch.
 c. *I'd like any coffee, please. (Radford 2009:71)

As is well known, the distribution of words like *any* is quite restrained. Thus, what the data in (52) show is that *any* cannot be used in positive declarative sentences. Modern grammarians, or syntacticians call words such as *any* **polarity items**. In addition, concerning their restricted distribution, they point out that polarity items are required to have appropriate "licensers." For instance, *no* and *if* are such licensers in the data in (52). What is the precise relationship between the two, that is, polarity words and their licensers? At first glance, it appears that the licenser must precede the polarity word (let us call this the **precedence condition**), in view of the ungrammaticality of the following sentence, which

61) Note the c-command domain of *he*, which is marked by a closed dotted line.

(i)

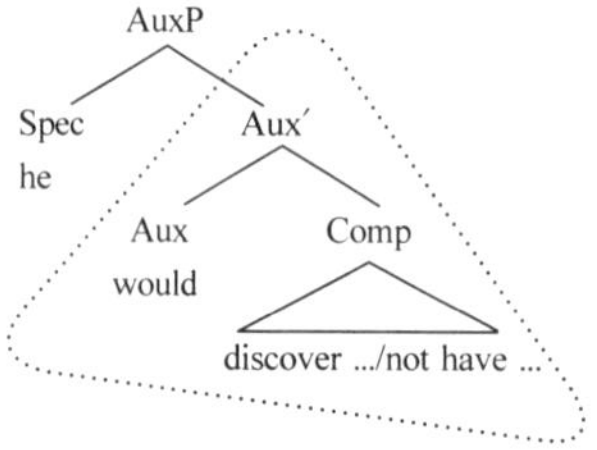

shows a striking contrast with the grammaticality of the sentence in (52a).

(53) *Anybody will complain about **nothing**.

However, the vulnerability of such a constraint is confirmed by the following pair of examples due to Radford (*ibid.*:72).

(54) a. The fact that he has resigned **won't** change anything.
b. *The fact that he **won't** resign will change anything.

The precedence condition predicts that both of the examples will be acceptable, contrary to fact. On the other hand, the following condition based upon the hierarchical relationship between a polarity item and its licenser seems to be sufficient to explain all the contrastive acceptability observed in the above data.

(55) **The Polarity Condition**
A polarity word must be c-commanded by a proper licenser.[62)]

Although there are many other kinds of data supporting the hierarchical analysis of English syntactic structures, suffice it to say that these two pieces of evidence justify it.

Before completing the present chapter, let us summarize the

62) In (52a), the subject *nobody* c-commands all the other elements in the sentence. Likewise, *if* c-commands everything contained in *anyone ... me* in (52b). (See section 5.6 for a structural analysis of an *if*-clause.) Consequently, the use of *anything/anyone* is acceptable. What about the data in (54)? The c-command domain of *won't* in (54a) and (54b) is *change anything* and *resign*, respectively. Hence the contrast in acceptability follows.

discussion so far.

a. Phrases other than the VP have a three-level projection (let us disregard adjuncts at the moment).

① minimal projection (=Head) X(=X^0) > intermediate projection X' > maximal projection XP(=X")

The whole projection can be generated by combining the following phrase structure rules.

② a. XP → Specifier + X'(XP consists of Specifier plus X'.)

b. X' → X + Complement (X' consists of X plus Complement.) (This can be stated conversely: A head X projects into the intermediate projection X' by merging with the complement. The intermediate projection X' projects into the maximal projection XP by merging with the specifier.)

③ The resulting structure can be represented by means of a tree diagram.

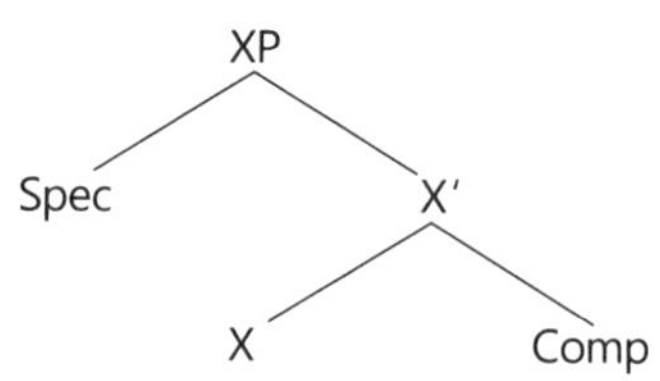

The syntactic system using the above PS rules and tree diagram is called X' theory/syntax. X' theory can be regarded as a great step toward simplifying the analysis of the English sentence structures. Thus, all the English sentences are generated by the rule schema in ②, and all their syntactic structures can be represented by means of the skeletal tree structure in ③.

b. Sentences can be analyzed as AuxPs.

If an auxiliary and a VP are merged, the auxiliary plays the role of the head. In addition, the subject of the sentence can be considered the specifier of the AuxP. As a consequence, the sentence can be analyzed as AuxP.

c. The VP is peculiar in that it appears to lack a specifier.

In the next chapter we will attempt to resolve the puzzle described in c.

Exercise 1 If X imposes some (semantic and / or formal) restrictions on Y when the two merge, we say that X selects Y. For instance, the verb *sing* restricts the range of its object. Thus, *the timber*, *a squirrel*, *Mary* cannot be chosen as the object of *sing* (*sing {songs / the opera / *the timber / *a squirrel / *Mary}*), since it does not allow them. Now in the case of the merger of *will* and *sing a song* which selects the other?

Exercise 2 What is the core head in each of the following expressions? In other words, what is the word characterizing each phrase as a whole? (Note that on our analysis the sentence is an AuxP.)

(1) all the interesting books about butterflies
(2) the clothes in the wardrobe
(3) John has hated his uncle's dog greatly.

In addition, indicate its specifier, complement, and adjunct, if any.

Exercise 3 Why does the complement merge with the head before the specifier does? More generally, what does it mean that X has priority over Y in merging with the head H?

Exercise 4 Consider the following data, focusing on the underlined parts.

(1) a. a book about English with a red cover
b. the teacher of art with mustache

In (1a, b), the underlined parts each modify the noun head preceding them. However, their relationships with the head are not quite the same. This can be seen from the ungrammaticality of the following data, where the order of the modifiers has been changed.

(2) a. *a book with a red cover about English
b. *the teacher with mustache of art

How can you explain the ungrammaticality?

Exercise 5 Observe the following data carefully. How can you explain the uses of reflexives in English? Show how the hierarchical relationship between reflexive pronouns and their antecedents plays an important role in explaining the behavior of reflexives.

(1) a. *The presidential candidate has been proud of him.
b. The presidential candidate has been proud of himself.
c. *Himself has been proud of the presidential candidate.
d. *Supporters of the presidential candidate has been proud of himself.

Exercise 6 As repeatedly pointed out, semantic closeness among syntactic elements seems to be reflected in their syntactic structure. Thus, semantically closer elements tend to be merged prior to less close elements. Let us call this the **syntax-semantics correlation principle**. This principle can be shown to apply to adjuncts as well: inner adjuncts are more closely connected to a head than outer adjuncts. Observe the following data, paying special attention to the underlined parts.

(1) a. Police will probably investigate the incident very closely.
b. Police will probably very closely investigate the incident.
c. *Police will very closely probably investigate the incident.
d. *Police will probably investigate very closely the incident.
e. What police will probably do is very closely investigate the incident.
f. *What police will very closely do is probably investigate the incident.

Can you explain why (1c, d, f) are unacceptable in striking contrast to the others? It would be helpful to draw the tree diagram for the sentence in (1a).

Exercise 7 In the text we have shown that tree structures can be generated by phrase structure rules. Write the PS rules for generating the tree in (49).

Exercise 8 Look at the following tree diagram and answer the questions.

(1)

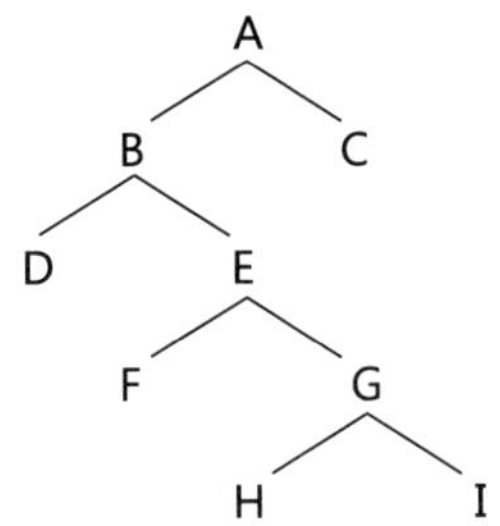

a. What is the root node?

b. What is the sister of C?

c. State the node(s) c-commanded by B.

d. Circle the c-command domain of D.

e. State all the nodes that are immediately dominated by E.

f. If E is assumed to be F', what is the function of G, and what about D's function?

g. How many constituents does the tree contain?

h. What is the smallest constituent containing F and H together?

i. State all the nodes dominated by E.

j. What is/are dominated by D?

Chapter 4
Extending X′ Syntax: TP and the VPISH

In chapter 3, we extended our syntactic analysis of English sentences. The results are as follows. First, we have discovered that all phrases are composed in a step-by-step fashion. The head X (X=N, A, P, Adv, or Aux) first merges with the complement, forming the intermediate projection X′. The intermediate projection in turn merges with the specifier, resulting in the maximal projection X″ or XP. In addition, one or more adjuncts can be adjoined to X′ or XP. What is more intriguing about our analysis is that it allows the sentence or clause to be analyzed as a sort of phrase, like NP, PP, AP, etc. More specifically, the sentence or clause is now analyzed as AuxP and the subject of the sentence/clause is assumed to be the specifier of AuxP. Thus, on our analysis, the sentence or clause is not idiosyncratic at all, unlike in traditional grammar.

However, our analysis is far from complete in some respects. First, the VP seems to be exceptional in that it appears to have no specifier. This is very unsatisfactory from the viewpoint of theoretical economy or elegance. If it is really true that only the VP lacks the specifier position, unlike the other phrases, it will make children's acquisition of English more complicated than otherwise. Therefore, we need to closely examine whether there is no room for permitting the specifier position for the VP as well. Another issue that is raised concerning our analysis is: how do we analyze sentences without auxiliaries if we assume that the sentence is AuxP? In this chapter we will try to answer these two questions.

4.1 The category T(ense)

Let us address the second question first: how do we analyze sentences without auxiliaries if we assume that the sentence is AuxP? This question may seem very perplexing because it appears to be simply impossible to analyze sentences without auxiliaries as AuxPs. However, before discarding the AuxP analysis of the sentence, let us consider some example sentences without auxiliaries.

(1) The old woman missed her husband.

(2) Jake plays football on Sundays.

(3) Park LOVES you.[63)]

Apparently, these three sentences contain no auxiliaries. Consequently, it would seem that they must be analyzed as VPs rather than AuxPs.

At this point it would be helpful to consider what meanings auxiliaries express. The following are typical examples of sentences containing auxiliaries.

63) Capital letters indicate a word with emphatic stress.

(4) The old woman will miss her husband.

(5) Jake has played football on Sundays for ten years.

(6) Park must be happy.

In (4), the auxiliary *will* adds future meaning to the verb. In other words, it expresses the time of the event denoted by the verb. In (5), the auxiliary *has* (together with the past participle form of the verb) conveys the perfect aspectual meaning. Lastly in (6), *must* expresses the certainty of Park's being happy. Based upon examples like these, we may conclude that auxiliaries are used to add temporal and/or aspectual meanings to the verb or to denote the possibility of the event expressed by the verb.

What about the sentences without auxiliaries in (1)-(3)? Despite non-occurrence of any auxiliaries in these sentences, they do contain temporal, aspectual, or modal meaning, as is obvious from the following glosses.[64)]

(1) The old woman missed her husband.
'The old woman miss her husband' + 'past time'

(2) Jake plays football on Sundays.
'Jake play football on Sunday' + 'present time, habitual aspect'

(3) Park LOVES you.
'Park's loving you is really certain'

Consequently, it is quite plausible to assume that (1)-(3) also contain some elements corresponding to auxiliaries. Can you

64) Note that the verbs in the glosses do not contain the suffix *-s*, since they are tenseless.

separate those "auxiliary" elements from them? Needless to say, they must be the inflectional tense suffixes *-ed* and *-s* contained in *missed, plays,* and *LOVES.*[65] Now if we isolate them from the verbs, they can be represented as follows. (Note that the inflectional tense suffixes are placed *before* the verb in order that their locations can be matched with the locations of the auxiliaries.)

(7) The old woman **-ed** miss her husband.

(8) Jake **-s** play football on Sundays.

(9) Park **-s** LOVE you.

We now have every reason to unify the inflectional tense suffixes and auxiliaries into the same category. But what category do we assign to this seemingly hybrid group: *can, must, will, may, -s,* and *-ed*? Interestingly, the modal auxiliaries are never used as **non-finite/tenseless** forms. Thus, there are no forms like **to can*, **be canning*, **have could.* This means that they always contain an (invisible) inflectional **tense** suffix. Accordingly, we will categorize this hybrid group as **T**(ense) from now on.[66] As a result of this categorization, both the sentence in (4) and that in (1) are analyzed as TP, as illustrated below.

65) More precisely speaking, the 'certainty' meaning of *LOVES* comes from both the suffix *-s* and the emphatic stress laid on *LOVES*. Here suffice it to say that inflectional suffixes are necessary to express certainty of a proposition.

66) A careful reader might suggest that modal auxiliaries and inflectional tense suffixes can be categorized as I(nfl) instead of T(ense), since they contain **inflectional** suffixes. Actually, some syntacticians categorize them as **I**(nfl). For them, then, the sentence is analyzed as **IP**! So don't be perplexed if you come upon terms like I, I′, and IP in the syntactic literature.

(10)

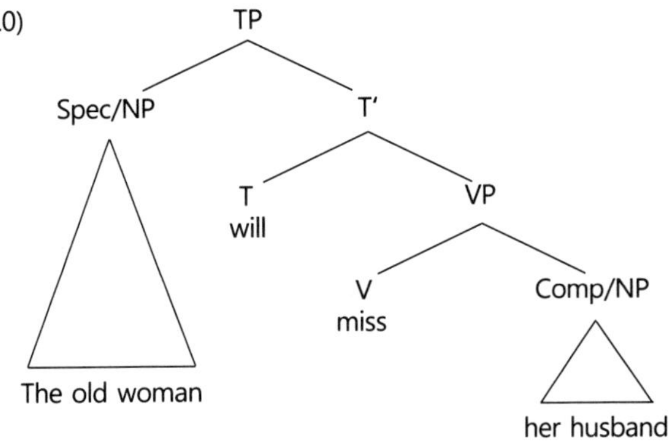

(11)

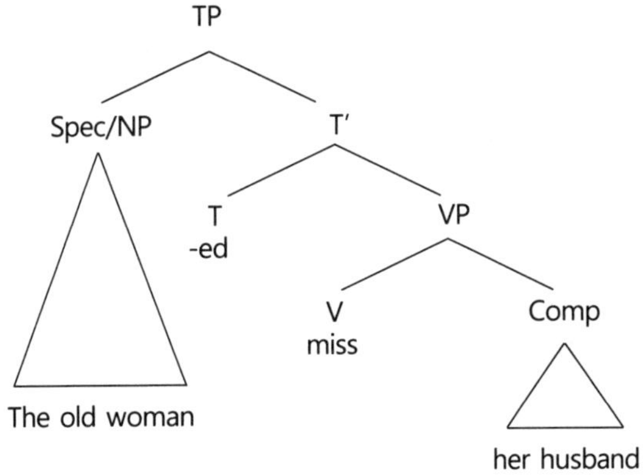

In addition, if we extend our analysis to all finite clauses, including the sentences in (1)-(6), they can generally be analyzed in conformity with the following structure.

(12)

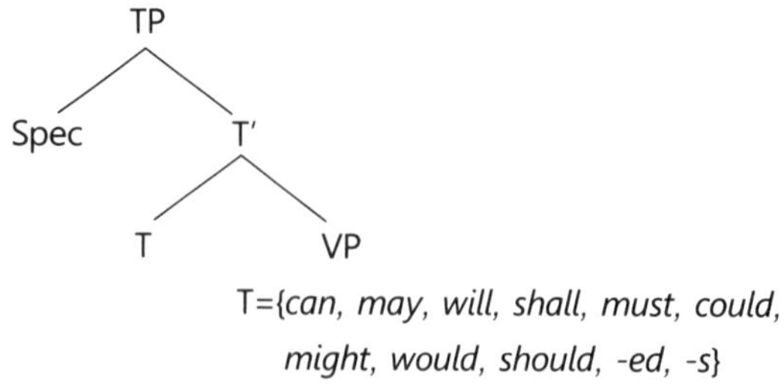

4.2 The infinitive marker *to*

The above-mentioned generalized analysis of finite clauses might inspire curiosity about how to analyze non-finite clauses, for instance, the ***to*-infinitive** clause. Let us observe the following example.

(13) The president wanted the secretary of state to visit Egypt as soon as possible.

According to the analysis proposed above, the main clause *The president wanted ... as possible* is analyzed as follows:

(14)

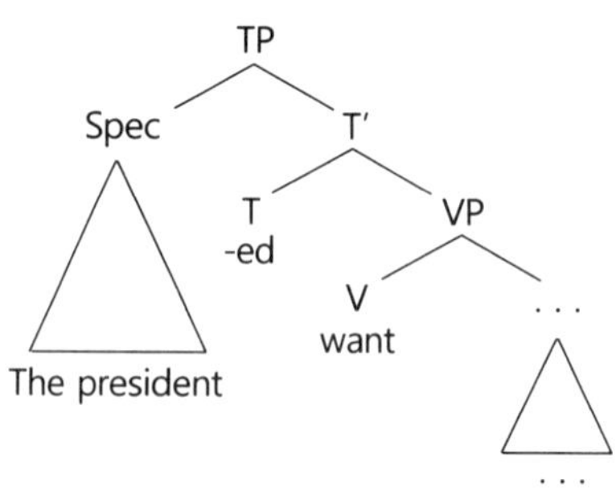

Now, what about the subordinate clause *the secretary of state to visit Egypt ...?*[67] To analyze its structure precisely, we first need to categorize the **infinitive marker *to***. What is its category? As a matter of fact, the infinitive marker *to* has been a knotty problem as far as its categorial status is concerned. Superficially, it looks like a preposition, since it is spelt like the preposition *to*. Actually, some traditional grammarians treated it as a preposition. However, we cannot accept such a view, since the **selectional** properties of the two are quite different, as evidenced in the following pair.

(15) a. We wanted *to* {meet/*meeting} you soon.
b. We were looking forward *to* {*meet/meeting} you soon.

As the data in (15) show, the infinitive marker *to* selects the infinitive form of the verb while the preposition *to* selects the *-ing* form of the verb. Now how can we resolve this conundrum?

The AuxP analysis of the clause helps us address the problem. Observe the following pair of sentences.

(16) a. I requested that Bill should send the package back at once.
b. I requested Bill to send the package back at once.

What we notice from the above data is that the infinitive marker *to* is in parallel with *should*. This observation leads us to classify *to* as T(ense). Their categorial similarity can also be seen in their behavior in elliptical sentences.

67) The clause is defined as the syntactic unit composed of the (semantic) subject plus the predicate.

(17) a. Mary requested that Bill should send the package back, and I think that he *should* ø. (ø = send it back)
b. Mary requested Bill to send the package back, and I expect him *to* ø. (ø = send it back)[68)]

Like *should*, which belongs to the category T, the infinitive marker *to*, as a word in the T category, can stand alone, allowing the phrase following it to be elided. Thus, the T category consists of {the modal auxiliaries, *-ed*, *-s*, *to*}. From the discussion so far we draw the conclusion that all (finite as well as non-finite) clauses in English are taken to be TPs with a T category word as its head.

4.3 Semantic roles and the VP-Internal Subject Hypothesis

Now let us try to tackle our first question: does the VP really lack a specifier? As repeatedly pointed out, it would be desirable for us to be able to argue that the VP must also contain a specifier position. Such an argument would enable us to subsume the VP structure under the generalized X′ syntax, together with the other kinds of phrases. The problem is how to procure justifications for such a claim.

Incidentally, there is another characteristic property that I have

68) Several scholars (e.g., Wierzbicka 1988, Bolinger 1977) claim that the infinitive marker *to* denotes 'futurity' or 'irrealis.' Hence, the classification of *to* as T is plausible in light of their characterization of its semantics.

neglected to mention concerning the internal structure of VP. Before mentioning it, we need to consider the structure of VP again. You may well be aware that the VP can contain adjuncts as well as complements. One of the things that I pointed out concerning the VP is that the complement is merged with the verb head prior to the adjunct(s), since the former is more closely related to the head than the latter. This is true of other phrases as well. Based upon these observations, we may formulate the following general principle.[69)]

(18) **The Syntax-Semantics Correlation Principle (SSCP)**
Semantically closer elements are merged prior to less close elements.

The SSCP explains the (un)acceptability of the word orders observed in the following data.

(19) a. I will discuss this problem in the afternoon.
b. *I will discuss in the afternoon this problem.

(20) a. They are going to look into the project after having lunch.
b. *They are going to look after having lunch into the project.

(19b) and (20b) are unacceptable because the adjunct is merged with the verb earlier than the complement is.

Now, it would be natural to ask a related question: which is semantically closer to the verb, the subject, which is located in the specifier position of TP, or the adjunct? Our intuition tells us that

69) We already mentioned this principle in exercise 6, chapter 3.

the subject seems to be closer. How can we justify our intuition that the (semantic) relationship between the subject and the verb is closer than that between the adjunct and the verb? First of all, like the complement, the subject is a necessary element for forming a sentence, whereas the adjunct is an optional one. Observe the following data.

(21) a. *John gave ø a book. (lacking a complement (= the indirect object))
b. *ø Gave Mary a book. (lacking the subject)
c. John gave Mary a book (**on the porch**). (optionality of the adjunct)

(22) a. *Bill loves ø. (lacking a complement (= the object))
b. *Loves a woman. (lacking the subject)
c. Bill loves a woman (**with all his heart**). (optionality of the adjunct)

(23) a. *ø Is raining. (lacking the subject)
b. It is raining (**heavily**). (optionality of the adjunct)

(24) a. *ø Became a doctor. (lacking the subject)
b. *Peggy became ø. (lacking a complement (=the subject attribute)
c. Peggy became a doctor (**in France**). (optionality of the adjunct)

Secondly, the **semantic role** of the subject is determined by the verb, whereas the semantic role of the adjunct is quite independent of the verb. This also testifies that the subject is closer to the verb than the adjunct is. Let us first observe the data showing that the subject is semantically dependent on the verb.

(25) a. Bill kissed Ann.
b. Bill received the letter from Ann.
c. Bill fell from the roof.

d. Bill liked soccer.

Bill inherently denotes a male person, but has no independent semantic role until it is merged with the verb. Once it merges with the verb, however, it takes a certain semantic role. What sort of semantic role it will receive is determined solely by the verb. For instance, *Bill* in each sentence in (25) is assigned a different semantic role by the verb, as noted in (25′).

(25′) a. Bill - kisser
b. Bill - recipient
c. Bill - the one who fell from the roof
d. Bill - soccer-lover

This means that the semantic relationship between the subject and the verb is very close.

In this connection, we may ask a more basic question: why on earth is the semantic role of the subject determined by the verb, but not by anything else? In order to answer this question, we need to consider what the basic functions of language are. It goes without saying that the most essential function of language is to communicate with others. What do we convey in communicating with others? Some information about every kind of situation happening around us. As a consequence, the sentence, the basic unit of linguistic communication, must describe some sort of situation occurring around us.

Basically, information about a situation consists of two essential elements—the **type of situation** (e.g., eating, loving, fighting, running, climbing, etc.) and the participant(s) of the situation (e.g., John, the banana, a girl, the dog, the river, a mountain, etc.). Situation types are expressed by the verb or *be*+adjective, and the participant(s) of a situation by NP(s). What kind of **participant role** an NP will have is determined by the type of situation expressed by the verb. Hence the verb's determination of the semantic/participant role of the subject, and the semantic closeness between the subject and verb!

Discussing semantic/participant roles of NPs in detail at this point might carry us far afield.[70] So let us discuss them briefly, taking some more examples in addition to those in (25).

(26) a. John walked to school.
b. John became famous.
c. John ate two bananas.
d. John handed Mary a copy of his book.
e. John put the book on the table.
f. The news shocked John.
g. The stone broke the window.

Although the participant roles of NPs (or PPs) seem to be as varied as the meanings of the verbs (e.g., kisser, walker, eater, recipient, thing given, location, etc.), they are believed to be classified into ten or so broad semantic categories, which are generally called **semantic roles** or **theta roles**. Regrettably, there is no standard list of semantic roles that all researchers have readily agreed to accept, but most of them seem to assume that at least the following list is

70) Interested readers are referred to Fillmore 1968, Gruber 1965, Kearns 2000.

needed to discuss the semantic roles of NPs.

(27) Semantic roles of NPs

a. **Agent**: the actor of an action
(**Bill** in (25a), **John** in (26a), (26c), (26d), (26e))

b. **Theme**: thing that undergoes or is affected by an action; thing that is in a certain state or undergoes certain change of state; thing that is moved to another place
(**Ann** in (25a), **the letter** in (25b), **two bananas** in (26c), **the book** in (26e), **John** in (26b), **Bill** in (25c) ...)

c. **Experiencer**: one who is emotionally or psychologically affected
(**Bill** in (25d), **John** in (26f))

d. **Instrument**: thing which denotes a means or instrument used to do something (**The stone** in (26g))

e. **Recipient**: one who receives something (**Bill** in (25b), **Mary** in (26d))

f. **Goal**: place to which something moves ((**to**) **school** in (26a))

g. **Source**: place from which something moves ((**from**) **Ann** in (25b))

If you examine the above examples and classification with great care, you might call into question the legitimacy of the classification, unsatisfied with it. Since detailed discussion might seem out of place, suffice it to say that every NP in a sentence has a semantic role and its semantic role is **assigned**/determined by the verb. The fact that the verb determines the semantic role of the subject proves that their semantic relationship is very close.

What about the adjunct? Can we prove that it is semantically less close to the verb, compared with the subject? Let us observe some sentences containing a temporal PP adjunct.

(28) a. Bill kissed Ann during his high school days.
b. Bill received the letter from Ann during his high school days.
c. Bill fell from the roof during his high school days.
d. Bill liked soccer during his high school days.

The adjunct PP *during his high school days* has an independent temporal meaning before it is merged with the verb. Even if it is merged with a variety of verbs, its meaning remains constant, which proves that it is semantically independent and expresses some additional, but not essential, information about a situation. (Hence it is called "adjunct.") It follows from this argument that the subject is semantically closer to the verb than the adjunct is.

Given the **Syntax-Semantics Correlation Principle** in (18), we now expect the subject to merge with the verb prior to the merger of the adjunct with the verb. In reality, however, the subject position is a lot farther from the verb than the adjunct position, as can be seen from the following tree diagram. More specifically, note that the subject is placed in the specifier of TP outside of VP while the adjunct is placed within VP.

(29)

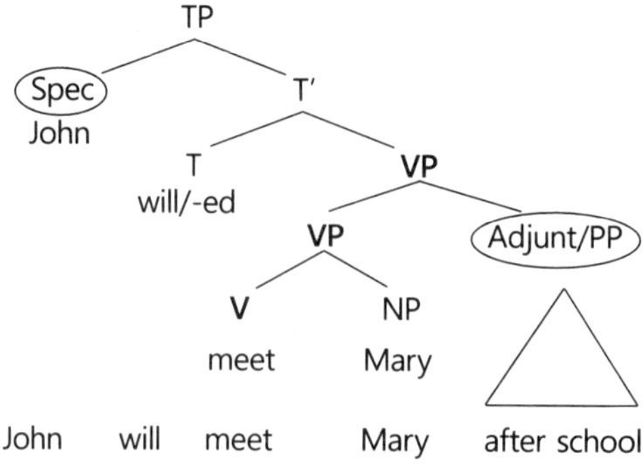

a. John will meet Mary after school
b. John -ed meet Mary after school

In other words, from a "syntactic" viewpoint, the adjunct is closer to the verb than the subject is, violating the **SSCP**.

We are now confronted with a dilemma: all sentences containing an auxiliary (for example, (29a)) violate the **Syntax-Semantics Correlation Principle** since their subject, placed in the specifier of TP, is *syntactically* less close to the verb than the adjunct, placed within VP, is, even though the former is *semantically* closer to the verb than the latter. What about sentences without an auxiliary (e.g., (29b))? If we assume that the analysis of all clauses as TPs is on the right track, sentences without an auxiliary also violate the **SSCP**.

Should we then abandon the intuitively plausible SSCP? It does not seem quite sensible. Instead, why don't we boldly propose a new hypothesis to the effect that the subject originates in the VP, although on the surface it is located in the specifier position of TP? (From now on let us use the abbreviated expression "Spec,XP" instead of the longer expression, "the specifier of XP," following current conventions in syntax. Be careful not to separate the comma (,) and XP.) If we accept that the subject originates within the VP, in which position of the VP does it originate? In the specifier position, in the complement position, or in the adjunct position? It cannot occupy the complement position, nor can it occupy the adjunct position, since the two positions are already occupied. Moreover, as we pointed out earlier, the specifier position of the VP is "strangely" non-existent. Now if we assume, in conformity with our new hypothesis, that the subject originates in the specifier position of VP, our two dilemmas—① the subject in Spec,TP violates the SSCP; ② the specifier position of VP is strangely non-existent—are resolved at the same time! Our new hypothesis is called the **VP-Internal Subject Hypothesis**, which can be formulated as follows.

(30) **The VP-Internal Subject Hypothesis (VPISH)**
The subject of the sentence/clause originates in Spec,VP.

Now, if we assume the **VPISH** to be basically correct, we should draw the structure of VP (and TP) as follows.

(31)

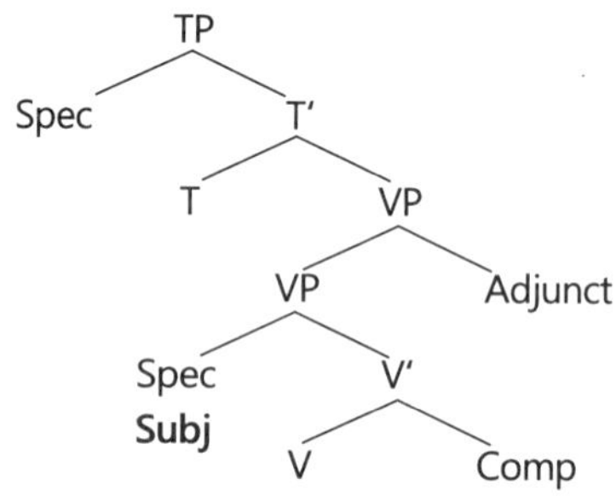

In the above tree diagram, V first merges with the complement, forming V′, which in turn merges with the subject, forming VP. The subject is placed in the specifier position in conformity with the X′ syntax format, and then the VP can optionally merge with the adjunct, which has the effect of expanding the VP. The tree diagram is fully consistent with the SSCP, since the syntactic structure properly reflects the relative semantic closeness of the subject and the adjunct with respect to the verb. Note that the semantically closer an element is to the verb, the deeper it is placed in the VP. Hence the depth of embedding of the basic elements in the VP is: complement 〉 subject 〉 adjunct.

As is evident from the above argumentation, the VPISH is obtained from the deductive approach to the structural analysis of VP: ① phrases other than VP have a specifier position, so by deductive reasoning it would be more natural for the VP to have a specifier position than otherwise; ② on the surface, the internal structure of VP is also idiosyncratic in light of the SSCP. The subject is placed outside VP while the adjunct is inside it, although the former is semantically closer to the verb than the latter. Thus, we deduce from the SSCP that the subject originates within VP.

In order to prove that a certain proposal is valid, we need to provide some empirical support for it in addition to **conceptual/ theoretical** arguments for it. Thus, it would be theoretically sounder if the VPISH is supported by some **empirical** evidence in addition to the above-mentioned conceptual arguments. In the next section we will turn to some empirical evidence supporting the VPISH.

Incidentally, in the course of our analysis of the syntactic structure of the sentence, you may have realized that the moment we seem to find the solution to a question, there ensue other issues. This typically happens in scientific research. It also shows that language can be a very intricate system whose detailed analysis is not an easy thing to do.

4.4 Empirical evidence for the VPISH

Adopting the VPISH implies that we take the subject, which is superficially found in Spec,TP, to be derived from Spec,VP, because the VPISH claims that the subject originates in Spec,VP. To take a concrete example, we claim that (32) is derived from (33).

(32) [$_{IP}$ John may [$_{VP}$ play golf on Saturday]].
(33) [$_{IP}$ may [$_{VP}$ John play golf on Saturday]].

What does it mean that (32) is derived from (33)? According to the VPISH, the subject *John* should stay in Spec,VP as represented in (33), but the sentence in (33), *May John play golf on Saturday,* cannot be used as it is. Instead, we should speak or write the sentence as represented in (32). What is the difference between the sentence in (32) and that in (33)? It is the relative linear order of the two words *John* and *may*. If we want to produce the correct sentence in (32) from the wrong one in (33), what process is needed? Clearly, we need to move *John* from Spec,VP to Spec,TP.

It might seem to be very simple to introduce a new kind of process in syntax, namely, **movement**. However, in scientific research we should be careful in introducing a new process or **theoretical construct** in order to explain a certain phenomenon. The reason is that scientific research aims to explain natural phenomena by means of the fewest possible devices. In this connection, it would be worthwhile to listen to what Einstein (1954), the greatest scientific genius of the 20th century, says.

(34) The grand aim of all science is to cover the greatest possible number of experimental facts by logical deduction from the smallest number of hypotheses or axioms.

What Einstein's remark quoted above implies for the present discussion is that we have to think over whether to postulate the new process of movement to account for syntactic phenomena. Incidentally, the following pair of sentences also seem to necessitate the invoking of a movement process.

(35) A: Yesterday I went to the E-mart with my mother.
B: (a) What did you buy?
A: (b) I bought some coffee and green tea.

To account for the placement of *what* in (35Ba) we have to postulate that it is moved from behind the verb *buy*. The postulation of movement is motivated as follows. The grammatical role of *what* in (35Ba) must be the object of the verb, as can be seen from A's response (35Ab) to B's question (35Ba). In general, the object of the verb occurs immediately behind the verb. Accordingly, it is quite natural that we assume that *what* in (35Ba) is moved from behind the verb *buy*.

Now that we have shown movement is **independently motivated** to account for a different phenomenon, namely, the formation of ***wh*-questions**, it is a theoretical free ride to utilize movement to deal with the data in (32)-(33). However, there remains a seemingly more difficult issue: how can we *prove* that the subject *actually* moves from Spec,VP to Spec,TP? Conceptually, postulating movement here seems to be very plausible, but who knows what actually happens in the brain of a native speaker of English when the sentence in (32) is formed? To our great surprise, however, we do have *empirical* evidence for the existence of the movement! Observe the following data.

(36) a. *All* the boys seem to appear to like ice cream.
b. The boys seem to appear to *all* like ice cream.
(Boeckx 2006:170)

(37) a. *All* the students should have been doing the exam at that time.
b. The students should have been *all* doing the exam at that time.
(Haegeman 2006:269)

Words like *all* are called **quantifiers** since they denote the quantity of the object expressed by the noun they modify. To give additional examples, *some, several, both, many, every*, etc. belong to quantifiers. Since quantifiers modify a nominal expression (let us call this the **associate** of the quantifier), forming an NP with it, they are expected to occur within the NP. Our expectation turns out to be real in (36a) and (37a). What is beyond our expectation (is this due to our being non-native speakers of English?) is that quantifiers can be separated from their associate and placed elsewhere in the sentence, as can be observed in (36b) and (37b). Confronted with the data in (36b) and (37b), we cannot simply conclude that the quantifier in them exists separately from its associate from the start, because the close semantic relatedness between the quantifier and its associate cannot be denied. This means that their relatedness must somehow be captured. How can we capture their relatedness in (36b) and (37b) despite their apparent separation? The easiest way to capture their semantic relatedness is to hypothesize that they originally formed an NP together and have been separated later. Where do you suppose they originate as an NP?

In answering this question, we can get great help from the VPISH. Let us first focus on the sentences in (37a, b). According to the VPISH, the subject *all the students* is expected to originate in Spec,VP, that is, immediately before the verb head *doing*. This means that the sentence in (37a) starts as that in (38) below.

(38) should have been all the students doing the exam at that time.

At the next stage of derivation, the NP in Spec,VP must move to Spec,TP.[71)] There are two ways available to execute movement of the NP in Spec,VP. One is to move the whole NP to Spec,TP, generating the sentence in (37a). The other is to move the associate, leaving the quantifier behind in Spec,VP. As a result of the second way of movement, the sentence in (37b) is generated.[72)]

---

71) The motivation for the movement of NP from Spec,VP to Spec,TP is generally believed to be the requirement that all finite clauses must have the subject. Note that the requirement is purely syntactic, considering that a meaningless, dummy element like *it* or *there* must fill in the subject position when no semantic element is required there. Observe the following relevant examples.

(i) a. *It* is warm today.
  b. *There* is a boy standing over there.

72) Can you take other examples in which the two ways of movement—one is to move the whole phrase and the other is to move part of it with the rest left behind—are available? When a preposition accompanies a *wh*-element, the *wh*-element can move alone with the preposition stranded or it can move together with it. The latter

As exemplified above, some quantifiers show alternative positioning in a sentence, and they are called **floating quantifiers.** When quantifiers are left behind separated from their associate NP, they are said to be "**stranded.**" The above examples show that the location of the stranded quantifier marks the original place of the subject NP, which strongly supports the validity of the VPISH.

The VPISH is also supported by the semantic properties of the examples in (36a,b). For ease of reference, we repeat the examples.

(36) a. *All* the boys seem to appear to like ice cream.
b. The boys seem to appear to *all* like ice cream.

The semantic role of *All the boys* in (36a) is the **experiencer**, which is **assigned** by the verb *like*. That the subject NP has little to do with the verbs *seem* and *appear* from a semantic viewpoint is evident from the paraphrase in (39) for the sentence in (36a).

(36) a. All the boys seem to appear to like ice cream.

(39) *It* seems that *it* appears that all the boys like ice cream.

Notice that the two verbs *seem* and *appear* can take the expletive *it* as their subject, which proves that they cannot assign a semantic role to their subject. This implies that from a semantic viewpoint the subject *all the boys* is more closely related to the verb *like* than to either of the two verbs *seem* and *appear*. Accordingly, it is very plausible to assert that *all the boys* originates as the subject

---

movement has been known as **pied-piping** since Ross 1967. cf. *He has no house which he can live in.* / *He has no house in which he can live.*

of the VP *like ice cream*, not as the subject of *seem* or *appear*. Our analysis is empirically supported by the example in (36b), where the stranded quantifier *all* occupies the position in which the subject *all the boys* was once located.

In the course of our argumentation, we mentioned the semantically null, expletive subject *there*. (See footnote 71.) Sentences containing it are usually called *there*-constructions. Now we will show that *there*-constructions also provide empirical evidence in support of the VPISH. Observe the following attested examples of the *there*-construction.

(40) Former Secretary of State Madeleine Albright said her impression after attending a recent Mitt Romney speech is that "there's just nothing going on" with the Republican presidential nominee.
(Sep. 30, 2012 First Read on NBC News.com)

(41) "To be honest, there is nothing really happening with Bhatts. None of us is in a hurry to come together for a film so soon."
(from http://www.glamsham.com)

If we omit *there* from the *there*-sentences in (40)-(41), we obtain the following.

(40′) ... just nothing is going on with the Republican presidential nominee.

(41′) To be honest, nothing is really happening with Bhatts.

If the VPISH is valid, the subject *nothing* in (40′)-(41′) is expected to have been moved from the specifier position of the VP: the place in front of *going*, and *really happening*. As a matter of fact, the *there*-constructions corresponding to (40′)-(41′) show that the subject can remain in its original position, causing the expletive subject *there* to fill Spec,TP, instead. Thus, the existence of *there*-constructions can be taken to support the VPISH empirically.

4.5 Summary

In this chapter we have tried to answer the questions raised from the results of the discussions in chapter 3. The posed questions and answers to them are:

a. If we analyze the sentence as AuxP, how should we analyze sentences without auxiliaries? We have shown that even auxiliariless sentences do contain meanings expressed by auxiliaries. More specifically, auxiliaries usually express tense-/aspect-related meanings or modal meanings, and auxiliariless sentences also contain these semantic elements. Thus, every finite sentence necessarily contains time-related meaning, which is expressed by the inflectional tense suffixes *-ed*, *-s* or *-ø*. Based upon these observations, we proposed that the modal auxiliaries and the inflectional tense suffixes be classified as T(ense). Given the new categorization, the sentence can be analyzed as TP. In addition, we showed that the *to*-infinitival clause can also be analyzed as TP, since the infinitive marker *to* behaves very similarly to the modal auxiliaries.

b. According to the analysis in chapter 3, the VP seems to be exceptional in that it appears to lack a specifier position. Is it a real gap or can the VP also be reanalyzed and subsumed under the X' theory format, like the other phrases? We set out to answer this question, assuming that its reanalysis may be better from a theoretic perspective. Furthermore, we have argued that the semantic relationship between the subject and verb is closer than that between the adjunct and verb. In order to maintain the **Syntax-Semantics Correlation Principle (SSCP)**, we have proposed the **VP-Internal Subject Hypothesis (VPISH)**, the basic tenet of which is that the subject originates in Spec,VP. By adopting the VPISH we have resolved the two conundrums simultaneously. The VPISH makes it possible to capture the semantic closeness between the subject and the verb, and eliminates the presumed exceptional property of the VP, by postulating a specifier position for the subject.

c. The above-mentioned motivations for the VPISH are conceptual and theoretical. If a hypothesis is to attain validity, there should be some empirical evidence provided for it. We have shown that the behavior of floating quantifiers and the existence of *there*-constructions strongly support the validity of the VPISH.

What are we going to do next? In dealing with the data which forced us to propose the VPISH, we pointed out the necessity of movement processes. For instance, to derive the canonical surface structure of the declarative sentence, whose subject is located in Spec,TP, we need to move the subject from Spec,VP to Spec,TP. Similarly, we need to postulate *wh*-movement for the derivation of *wh*-questions. In addition, we have not dealt with sentences with multiple auxiliaries, which will be shown to require movement processes. Let us discuss these problems in the next chapter.

Exercise 1 State the semantic role of each underlined part of the following sentences.

(1) An 11-year-old boy was hit by a tree branch this morning.
(2) Bill sent a birthday present to his brother.
(3) Someone broke the window with a stone.
(4) I received a letter from my uncle.
(5) Poseidon was greatly shocked at the news.
(6) This bus goes from New York to Chicago.
(7) We rolled down the hill.

Exercise 2 For each of the following sentences, make up a pair of interrogative sentences such that the underlined part can be the answer to the interrogatives. State the differences between each pair.

(1) I have been waiting for Max.
(2) My grandmother is looking after my younger brothers.
(3) Susan went shopping with Jane.

Next, combine each pair of the following sentences into a complex sentence by means of a relative clause. (You can only use relative pronouns containing *wh-*.) Note that there are two ways of composition.

(4) a. Judy has several friends.
b. She can depend on the friends.

(5) a. Do you have some foil?
b. I can wrap this fish in foil.

What are the similarities between *wh*-expressions and *wh*-relative pronouns?

Exercise 3 Transform each of the following sentences into the corresponding *there*-sentence.

(1) Several boys are playing on the ground.
(2) Many books are on the shelf.
(3) Thousands of houses were destroyed in the earthquake.

Now, observe the following set of examples carefully, and formulate a constraint on *there*-constructions.

(4) a. There is a book on the table.
b. There is no book on the table.
c. *There is that book on the table.
d. *There is John standing over there.

Chapter 5 Movement

Sentences are formed by combining more than one word. Accordingly, the process of **merger** is essential for generating sentences. However, merger alone is not sufficient for explaining the formation of sentences. Instead, the process of **movement** is also needed. For instance, *wh*-interrogative sentences are formed through the movement of *wh*-expressions to the clause-initial position. In this chapter we will discuss how movement applies to relevant structures.

5.1 T-lowering versus V-raising

If we adopt the VPISH and assume that the sentence is analyzed as TP, we can represent the structure of a concrete sentence without any auxiliary as follows.

(1)

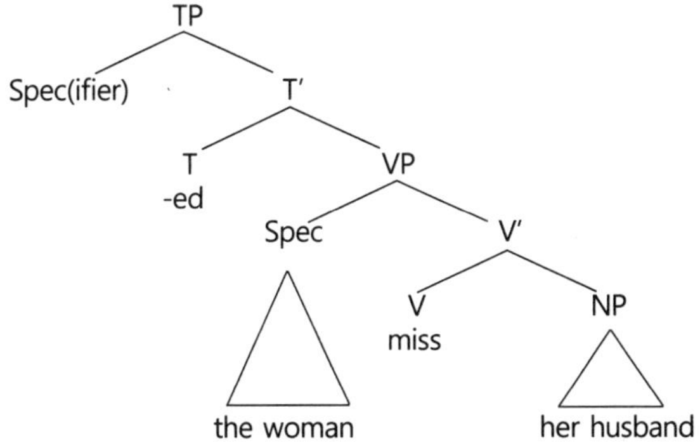

The representation in (1) is, however, problematic, since it does not match the sentence used in reality by native speakers of English. The actual sentence is: *The woman missed her husband* (but not **Ed the woman miss her husband*). In order to obtain the right result, we need to posit at least two processes. One is the movement of *the woman* to the specifier of TP, and the other the unification of *-ed* and the verb *miss,* which also seems to necessitate another kind of movement.

With respect to the first process, we may posit the following requirement.

(2) **The EPP**[73)]
Every finite clause must get its subject position filled by an overt, namely, visible/pronounceable element.

The EPP does not seem to be attributable to semantics, in view of examples like the following, which contain expletive elements like *it/there.*

(3) a. *(It) is cloudy outside.
b. *(There) were no trees here in my younger days.

Obviously, the EPP triggers the movement of the subject from Spec,VP to Spec,TP.

73) The EPP abbreviates the **Extended Projection Principle**. The subject is usually required by the semantics of the verb. Why then does the TP require the subject, despite there being no such semantic requirement in TP? Chomsky proposes that T(ense) is required to continue its projection until it reaches its maximal projection TP for purely syntactic reasons. This means that the TP is required to have its specifier position filled by an overt NP, as stated in (2) in the text. cf. footnote 71.

Now the remaining problem is how to obtain *missed* from *-ed* and *miss*. It seems to be straightforward to derive *missed* from *-ed* and *miss*, since typical past forms like *wanted* and *studied* are formed by *want* + *-ed* and *study* + *-ed*. In reality, however, things are not so simple; there are two ways to derive *missed* from the tree diagram in (1): ① the suffix *-ed* lowers onto the verb *miss* (**T-lowering**); ② the verb *miss* raises to the suffix *-ed* (**V-raising**). Which of the two is correct? There is one argument for the first alternative. Observe the following relevant data, paying special attention to the location of the adverb *often*.

(4) a. The lady has ***often*** enjoyed horse races.
    b. The lady ***often*** enjoyed horse races.
    c. *The lady enjoyed ***often*** horse races.

Apart from the fact that their T head positions are filled with different elements, (4a) and (4b) have the same base structure, as represented below.

(5)

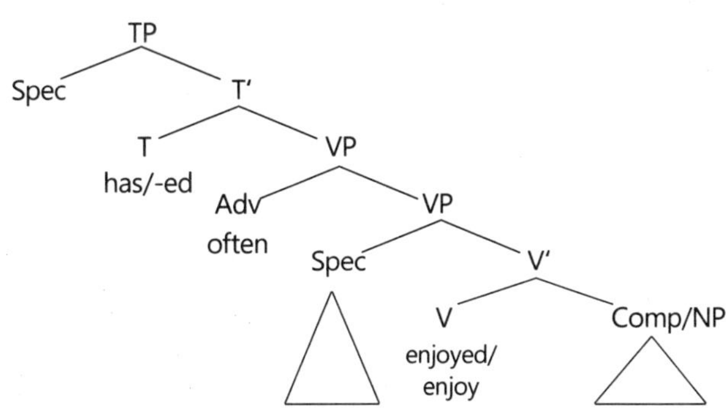

(4') a. has often the lady enjoyed horse races
     b. -ed often the lady enjoy horse races

At the next stage of derivation the EPP applies to this base structure, resulting in the following structure.

(6)

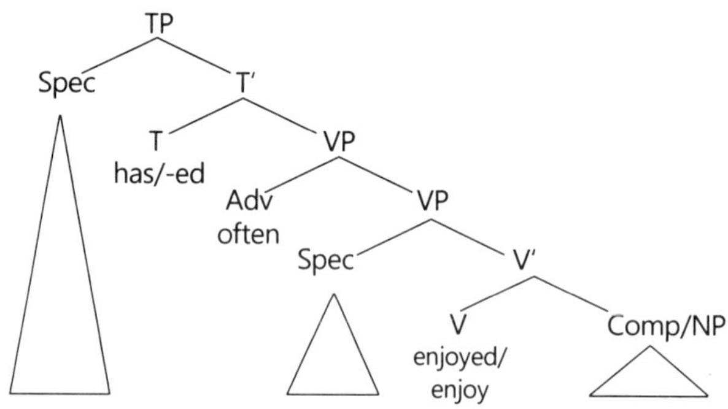

(4″) a. the lady has often ~~the lady~~ enjoyed horse races
b. the lady -ed often ~~the lady~~ enjoy horse races

In the case of (4a, 4′a, 4″a) no further step of derivation is needed. On the other hand, in the case of (4b), we have now arrived at a critical point. If the sentence did not contain the adverb *often*, T-lowering and V-raising would produce the same result. In contrast, when an adverb like *often* intervenes between the T head and the verb *enjoy*, the two processes produce different results, as shown below.[74)]

(7) a. T-lowering: The lady ~~-ed~~ often enjoy-ed horse races.
b. V-raising: *The lady enjoy-ed often ~~enjoy~~ horse races.

Thus, the contrast in grammaticality observed between (7a) and (7b) leads us to conclude that the T-lowering analysis is correct.

---

74) The copy with strikethrough represents the original copy before movement.

5.2 *Yes/No*-question formation

So far so good. Next, let us discuss a new type of sentence whose derivation also seems to involve movement. As is well known, declarative sentences are transformed into their corresponding interrogatives by inverting the subject with the first auxiliary. This is illustrated in the following examples.

(8) a. John can play the piano very well.
    b. Can John play the piano very well?

(9) a. Bill has climbed Mt. Everest with his university friends.
    b. Has Bill climbed Mt. Everest with his university friends?

Obviously, the subject and the (first) auxiliary change their places and accordingly traditional grammarians called the process the **subject-auxiliary inversion**. However, the naming of the rule is not sufficiently explicit, for there are three possible ways for the subject to invert with the auxiliary: ① the subject moves to the place behind the auxiliary; ② the auxiliary moves to the place in front of the subject; ③ the subject and the auxiliary move to each other's place. Whichever of the three processes we apply to (8a) and (9a), we obtain the same result.

Which is the correct one, then? In other words, which of the three actually occurs in the brain of a native speaker of English? We cannot decide until we run some crucial experiments with regard to the relevant examples. For instance, we can run an experiment on the sentence in (8a). How should we do it? The situation we are confronted with is this. On the surface A and B exchange their places. But there are at least three possible ways for them to exchange their places. The problem is that we cannot decide offhand which of the three is the correct one. If we arrange A and B consecutively, the results of the three different processes are the same, making our efforts to choose one fruitless.

Now what happens if we insert X between A and B? In that case, the results of the three operations are certainly different, as shown below.

(10) A X B
① A moves to the place behind B → **X** B A
② B moves to the place in front of A → B A **X**
③ A and B exchange their places → B **X** A

Consequently, we have only to insert some expression that does not make the resultant sentence ungrammatical. For instance, we can insert *probably* between the subject and the auxiliary, like the following.

(11) John probably will attend the meeting.

If we execute the three operations to the sentence in (11), we obtain the following results, which lead us to conclude that the second option is the correct one.

(12) a. *Probably will John attend the meeting?
b. Will John probably attend the meeting?
c. *Will probably John attend the meeting?

A careful reader would be aware that our research method is very similar to that used in natural sciences. Scientists studying natural phenomena often run experiments, especially when they cannot decide which is the most appropriate among the possible explanations for some phenomena. Likewise, syntacticians run experiments to check whether their hypotheses are empirically supported. Fortunately, whenever they want, they can get native speakers' judgments about newly manipulated or invented sentences, since native speakers possess the ability to judge the grammaticality of those examples in light of the grammatical rules stored in their brain. For instance, if syntacticians present the manipulated examples in (12a-c) on the basis of the sentence in (11), native speakers instantly judge the grammaticality of (12a-c), and help the researchers choose one hypothesis over the others.

As a result of the argumentation using the invented examples, we obtain the following rule for forming *yes/no*-questions in English.

(13) **The *Yes/No*-Question Formation Rule**
In order to form a *yes/no*-question from a corresponding declarative sentence, move the first auxiliary to the place in front of the subject.

5.3 *Do*-support

According to the ***Yes/No*-Question Formation Rule** in (13), a declarative sentence is required to contain one or more auxiliaries to be changed into an interrogative sentence. This is definitely not the case, however, in view of the existence of examples like the following.

(14) a. John played the guitar in the concert hall.
b. Did John play the guitar in the concert hall?

What attracts our attention in the above examples is the fact that auxiliariless sentences necessitate the support of the so-called **dummy auxiliary** *do/does/did* when changed into the corresponding interrogatives. Thus, we face a new question of why an appropriate form of *do* must be supported (hence the term ***do*-support**) in forming interrogative sentences from auxiliariless sentences.

In order to answer this question, we first need to analyze the structure of the sentence in (14a). On our analysis proposed in chapter 4, the base structure of (14a) is represented as follows.

(15)

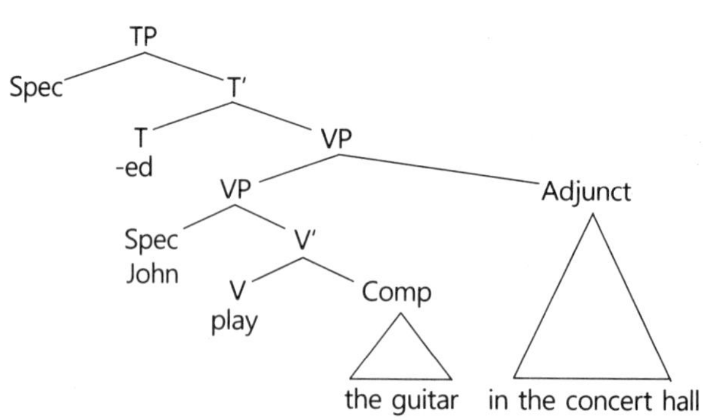

Based upon the earlier discussion we assume that *-ed* belongs to the T category together with auxiliaries. In other words, we can unify the inflectional tense suffixes and (first) auxiliaries as T. As a consequence, at this point, we can revise the *Yes/No*-Question Formation Rule as follows, substituting T for the first auxiliary.

(16) **The *Yes/No*-Question Formation Rule** (Revised)
In order to form a *yes/no*-question from a declarative sentence, move the T head to the left of the subject.

Applying the rule in (16) in forming an interrogative sentence for (14a), we front *-ed* to the left of the subject *John,* in Spec,TP,[75)] which results in the following representation.

(17)

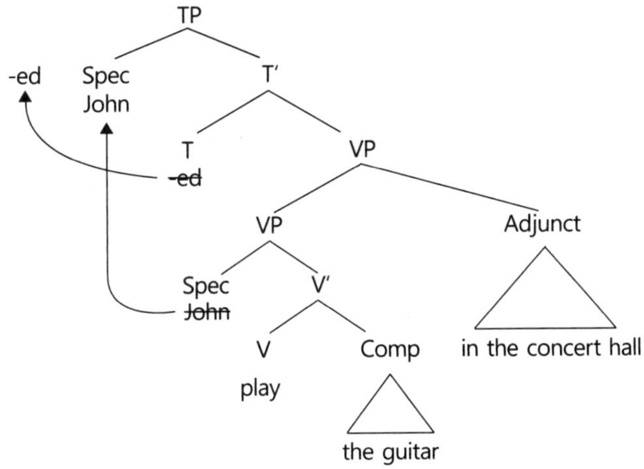

75) Note that at the stage of the movement of *-ed,* the subject *John* has already moved to Spec,TP. Although we need to discuss why the subject moves prior to *-ed,* let us leave this problem aside for the moment.

However, the resultant sentence is not acceptable (**Ed John play the guitar in the concert hall?*), because it cannot be pronounced as it is. As is widely acknowledged, suffixes like *-ed* cannot stand alone, and must attach to something else. In addition, since *-ed* is a verbal suffix, it must attach to the verb *play*. As it turned out in the foregoing that English allows T-lowering, but not V-raising, there is no choice but to make *-ed* lower onto the verb *play*. Unexpectedly, however, the lowering of *-ed* results in an unacceptable sentence as a canonical question.[76)]

(18) *John played the guitar in the concert hall?

As a matter of fact, if the result were accepted as a grammatical sentence, it would be very deplorable. The reason for this is that the form of a declarative sentence and its corresponding interrogative form would be identical and as a result there could be no proper communication at all! In this connection, we need to heed what Haegeman (2006:178) says.[77)]

> In order to signal interrogative force, we move the content of I to the left of the subject. ... If we were to lower it [= the inflectional morpheme *-ed*] into VP and insert it onto V, then we would no longer signal interrogative force.

---

76) Of course, this sentence can be acceptable as a question in special context like the following.

(i) John played the guitar in the concert hall? I can't believe it.

77) Note that Haegeman's I corresponds to our T. See footnote 66.

In other words, the lowering of *-ed* should be blocked; otherwise there would be no way to indicate that the sentence in question has interrogative force.

The dilemma is that *-ed* is a bound morpheme, so it cannot stand alone in front of the subject. Nor can the verb raise to *-ed*, since that is not allowed in English. Now how can we resolve this dilemma? *Do*-support in front of *-ed* enables us to rescue the stranded *-ed*. Observe the representation below.

(19)

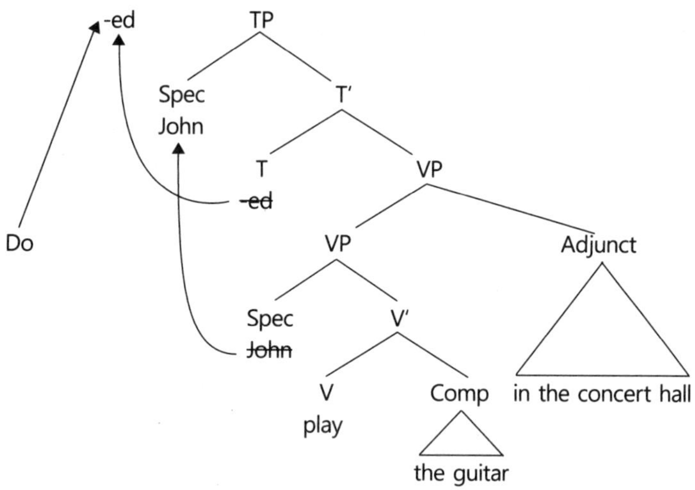

Do-ed is finally spelled/pronounced as Did/[did], resulting in an acceptable interrogative sentence.

5.4 *Wh*-questions

Since we have analyzed *yes/no*-questions, let us turn to another type of question, that is, *wh*-questions. First, observe the following examples.

(20) Where can I find Aesop's fables?

(21) What did you eat for lunch?

In order to derive these *wh*-questions correctly, we need to postulate their base structures properly. As revealed in the discussion of *yes/no*-questions, the elements preceding the subject do not originate there. Rather, they are likely to originate somewhere within the VP.

How can we ensure where they originate? Possible responses to the questions provide the clue.

(22) A: Where can I find Aesop's fables?
B: You can find them in the Children's Book section.

(23) A: What did you eat for lunch?
B: I ate a regular cheeseburger for lunch.

From the above two pieces of dialogue we may notice that the *wh*-words correspond to the PP adjunct and the object NP, respectively. Based upon this observation, we can suggest (24) and (25) as the base structures of (20) and (21), respectively.

(24)

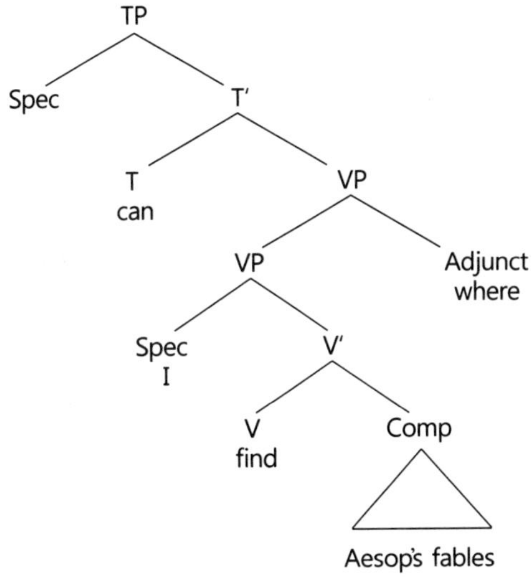

(25)

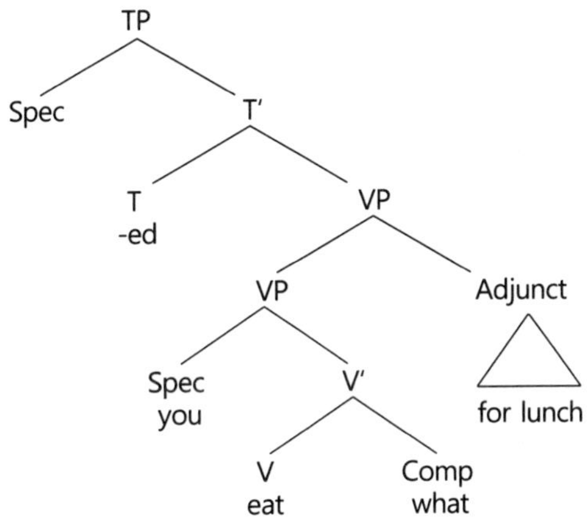

What happens at the next stage of derivation? The EPP forces the subjects *I* and *you* to move to Spec,TP, producing the following intermediate structures.

(26)

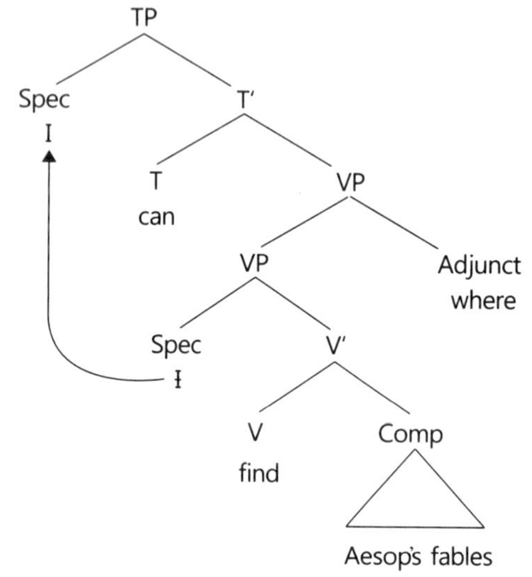

(27)

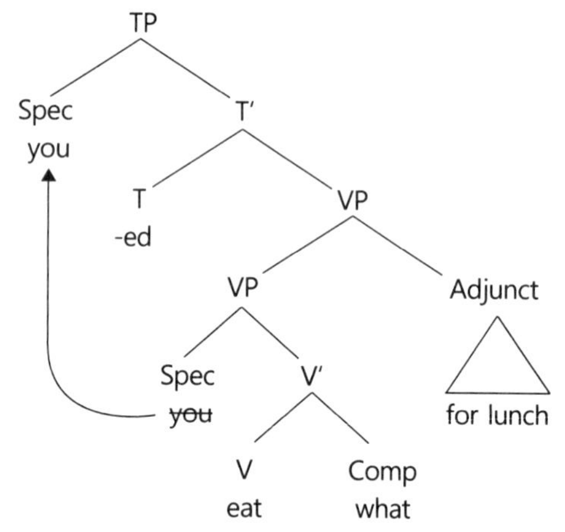

Now we have reached (almost) the final step of the derivation of *wh*-questions. What happens in the final step? The *wh*-expression and the T head move to the front of the subject, and as a result, we obtain the following structures.

(28)

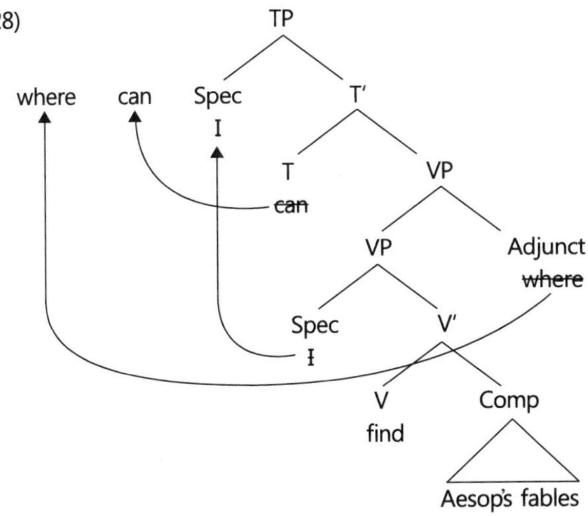

(29)

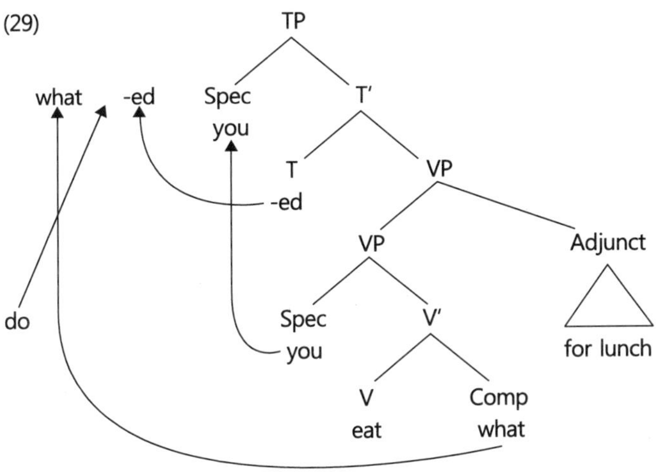

The structure in (28) needs no further adjustment. On the other hand, that in (29) requires *do*-support to rescue the stranded suffix *-ed*, resulting in *What did you eat for lunch?*—a desired result.

Are we now satisfied with the analysis? It seems to be too

early to pop the champagne. Take a careful look at the tree diagrams in (28) and (29). Do you notice any problems with them? No? You should find them yourself. Postponing discussion of the presumed problems until you discover them, let us turn to a new issue.

5.5 Multiple auxiliaries

So far we have dealt with the derivation of sentences with one auxiliary and those with none. However, it is well known that English allows up to four auxiliaries to precede the main verb, which is exemplified below.

(30) The Israeli soldier *may have been being* tortured by Palestinian terrorists.

(31)	may	-	have	-	been	-	being
	modal		perfect		progressive		passive

Here let us pose a question: how is the sentence in (30) derived under the VPISH?

Before addressing this question, we had better first deal with the problem of the categorization of various auxiliaries. Up to now we have categorized *may* as T. What about the other auxiliaries, that is, the perfect *have*, the progressive *be*, and the passive *be*? The motivation for the categorization of the modals, say, *may,* as T is the fact that they always contain an (invisible) tense suffix. But that is not always true of the other auxiliaries, as can be seen in the following data.

(32) a. The dog has barked for 10 minutes. (*have* + *-s*)
b. The dog seems to have barked for 10 minutes. (infinitival *have*)

(33) a. The Israeli soldier was beaten hard by the terrorists. (*be* + *-ed*)
b. The Israeli soldier had been beaten hard by the terrorists. (nonfinite *been*)

So it does not seem to be reasonable to classify the other auxiliaries as T, as in the case of the modal auxiliaries and tense suffixes. Taking this difference between the two groups into account, let us classify auxiliaries other than the modals as Aux.[78)]

Now how do we represent the structure of (30)? Since representing the structure of the sentence in (30) could possibly involve many complications owing to the passive voice, which we cannot explicate here in detail, let us try to represent the (surface, not base) structure of its active counterpart below.

(34) Palestinian terrorists may have been torturing the Israeli soldier.

78) If there is more than one auxiliary following the modal or tense suffix, let us differentiate those auxiliaries as Aux_1, Aux_2, etc.

(35)

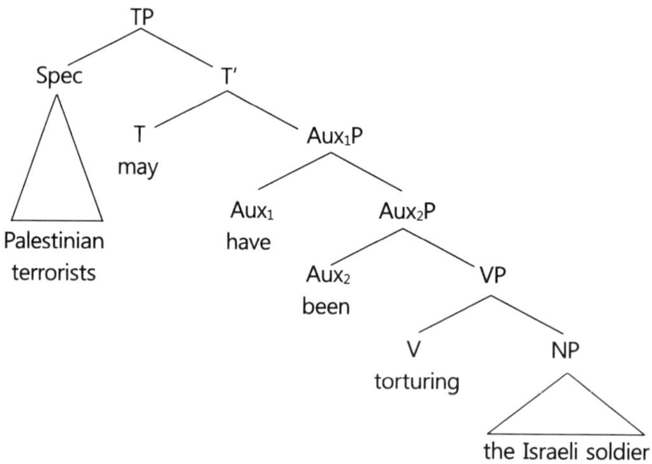

While observing the tree diagram in (35), careful readers might ask at least three questions. What do you think they are? Question one: on what grounds do we treat Aux as a head when it merges with the VP or another AuxP? Question two: does the AuxP also contain a specifier position (which is not postulated in (35))? Question three: where does the subject originate, in Spec,VP, Spec, Aux_2P, or Spec,Aux_1P (if we assume that the latter two positions exist)? Let us attempt to answer these questions in turn.

Obviously, Aux_2 is the progressive *be*. When Aux_2 merges with the VP *torturing the Israeli soldier*, which is the head of the merger? Two pieces of evidence justify the claim that Aux_2 is the head. First, while *tortur(ing) the Israeli soldier* can form an independent phrase by itself, the auxiliary *be* cannot stand alone. It must merge with a VP. Second, the auxiliary *be* selects the specific form of the following verb, namely, the *-ing* form. For these two reasons we assign the status of a head to the progressive *be*.

Almost the same reasoning applies to Aux_1 and Aux_2P. *Be torturing the Israeli soldier* does not require any auxiliary whereas the perfect auxiliary *have* requires an AuxP containing a VP or a bare VP. Moreover, it selects the past participle form of the following (auxiliary or main) verb.

Our second question is concerned with the (non-)existence of the specifier position of AuxP. Incidentally, in our earlier discussion we mentioned that if certain research is to be scientific, it should have several properties. One of them is concerned with simplicity. To put it shortly, as Hornstein *et al.* (2005:8) point out, "more is worse, fewer is better."[79) As an illustration, we can review our analysis of VP. As you might recall, we attempted to analyze the VP as having three levels of projection (V, V′, VP), by analogy with the projection of NP, PP, AP, AdvP and TP, despite the lack of any direct evidence for such an analysis. After all, we proved that our analysis is supported empirically as well as theoretically.

Now if we can extend the same approach to the AuxP, the phrase structure rules would be simpler than otherwise. In other words, if we assume that the AuxP also contains a specifier position, we can generate all sorts of phrases by using the general X′ syntax format. Thus, the conceptual argument seems to support the postulation of a specifier position for the AuxP, but what is at issue

79) The idea that fewer is better in scientific explanation is often referred to as **Occam's** (or **Ockham's**) **razor**, since the idea is attributed to "William of Ockham (c. 1285-1349) [, who] is remembered as an influential Roman Catholic philosopher and nominalist, ... The term razor refers to distinguishing between two hypotheses either by "shaving away" unnecessary assumptions or cutting apart two similar conclusions." (from Wikipedia, *s.v.* Occam's razor)

is whether there is any empirical evidence for such an analysis. Leaving this problem aside for a while, let us turn to the third question.

If we assume that the AuxP also has a specifier position in accordance with the above conceptual argument, where does the subject originate? In the sentence in (34) the subject *Palestinian terrorists* takes the semantic role of agent, that is, the role of torturer. This means that it receives its semantic role from the verb *torture*, not from either of the two auxiliaries. Consequently, we should choose Spec,VP as the place where the subject originates, which is completely consistent with the VPISH.

At this point there emerges another question: does the subject *Palestinian terrorists* raise from Spec,VP to Spec,TP in a single step, or does it raise in a step-by-step fashion, stopping by some intermediate position(s)? If the latter is true, what steps does the subject take? Is there any motivation for the choice between the two alternatives? Yes, there are at least two kinds of motivation! What do you think they are? One is conceptual, and the other empirical.

Do you remember that we have put the second question aside, assuming that the AuxP also has a specifier position? If the AuxP does have a specifier position, as we assume, that position must be filled by something. What is that something? Here we can kill two birds with one stone! As was pointed out previously, the canonical place-holder of the specifier position is the subject. As a consequence, we naturally expect that Spec,AuxP is filled by the subject. But on the surface there is nothing, let alone the subject. Where can we get the thing that not only fills Spec,AuxP but also plays the role of the subject? There seems to be no reason to rule out the possibility that the subject moving from Spec,VP stops by Spec,AuxP. If that should be true, we could kill two birds with one stone! This implies that we would prefer step-by-step derivations to one-fell-swoop derivations. In other words, the former are favored in terms of conceptual argument.

In addition, the fact that there is an empirical argument for the former (=step-by-step derivations) leads us to favor them over the latter. Observe the following data due to McCawley (1988:90; (36a) added for argumentation).

(36) a. *All* the neighbors must have been sleeping.
   b. The neighbors must *all* have been sleeping.
   c. The neighbors must have *all* been sleeping.
   d. The neighbors must have been *all* sleeping.

From a semantic viewpoint *all* modifies the subject *the neighbors*, which implies that *all* and *the neighbors* are merged together to form a single constituent *all the neighbors* in the base structure. Next, if the phrase as a whole moves from Spec,VP to Spec,TP, we get the sentence in (36a). If we take only this example into account, we cannot decide whether the subject moves to Spec,TP at one fell swoop, or it does so in a step-by-step fashion. On the other hand, if we are to account for the other examples in (36), we cannot but assume that *all the neighbors* moves from its base position, Spec,VP, toward its final destination, Spec,TP, in a step-by-step fashion. More specifically, when it moves toward Spec,TP, *all the neighbors* stops by every specifier position existing between Spec,TP and Spec,VP. In addition, there are two types of movement available. Either the whole phrase *all the neighbors* moves up to Spec,TP, or only *the neighbors* moves up to Spec,TP, leaving the quantifier *all* behind in one of the intervening specifier positions. In this way we can explain away the distributions of the floating quantifier *all* in the examples in (36). To conclude, sentences containing a floating quantifier can be considered to be compelling empirical evidence for the postulation of the specifier position in the AuxP as well as for the validity of the VPISH.

5.6 CP, and *wh*-movement revisited

On the surface, the subject of a clause occurs in Spec,TP. However, as the above-mentioned empirical as well as conceptual arguments have shown, it actually originates in Spec,VP and moves upward, filling all the intermediate specifier positions on its way to Spec,TP. The trigger for the upward movement of the subject from Spec,VP is the EPP: every specifier position of TP and AuxP must be filled by the subject.[80)]

Besides the movement of the subject, there are other movements motivated to account for the relationship between some pairs of

80) Note that the domain of application of the EPP is extended from TP to AuxP.

sentences. T-movement and *wh*-movement can be taken to be such examples. Observe the following data.

(37) a. John has recently received a letter from his friend.
    b. Has John recently received a letter from his friend?

(38) A: John returned from his trip to Europe yesterday.
    B: (a) What did he buy in Europe?
    A: (b) He bought a lot of postcards (in Europe).

Obviously, *yes/no* questions are formed by inverting the subject and the T head. We have previously claimed that the more accurate statement of the rule is this: T (e.g., *has* in (37)) moves to the left of the subject.

What happens in the case of *wh*-questions like (38Ba)? Considering that *a lot of postcards* in (38Ab) corresponds to *What* in (38Ba), *What* must function as the object of the verb *buy,* like *a lot of postcards*. This implies that *What* originates in the object position of *buy* in the base structure, as shown below.

(39)

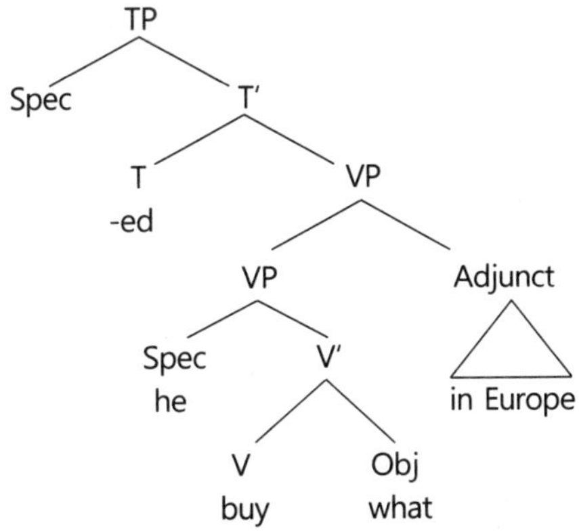

At the next stage of derivation, *he* moves to Spec,TP due to the EPP. What happens next? In order for the sentence in (38Ba) to be derived, two elements—*What* and *-ed*—are required to move. Concerning the movement of these two elements, I insisted in section 5.4 that you point out some problems. Can you now point them out?

If we try to move the two elements, we are likely to face at least two problems. First, why on earth do they move? Second, where exactly are the moved T and *wh*-expression located? Or how should we draw the lines connecting the two elements to the tree diagram? As a matter of fact, we should have asked the first question when analyzing the structure of the *yes/no*-question, since that construction also involves the movement of the T head. To change our question, why does the T head move at all in *yes/no*- and *wh*-questions? In other words, what triggers the movement of T?

In order to answer this question, we need to know that English sentences are classified into four types according to their semantic/ discourse functions: **declarative** sentences, **interrogative** sentences, **imperative** sentences, and **exclamative** sentences, as exemplified below.[81)]

(40) Toyota is recalling 1.53 million Avalon, Highlander and Lexus vehicles.

81) Some might suggest that negative sentences can be considered an independent type of sentences, but traditionally, they are not conceived as an independent type. The reason seems to be that their word order and verbal form are not distinct, compared with those of the four types. Thus, they are included in the declarative type.

(41) Is Toyota recalling 1.53 million Avalon, Highlander and Lexus vehicles?

(42) Recall all those cars having problems with the engine.

(43) What a wonderful car this is!

Following conventions, let us say that each type of sentence has its own **sentential** or **illocutionary force**.[82)] More specifically, the sentences in (40), (41), (42), and (43) are said to have declarative force, interrogative force, imperative force, and exclamative force, respectively.

On what basis do we judge that a sentence has specific illocutionary force? Apart from imperatives, (which we will not discuss here,) our judgment about illocutionary force of a sentence rests on its word order, especially, the relative position of its subject. Summed up below are the relative positions of the subject with respect to other elements.

(44) Illocutionary force and relative positions of the subject

illocutionary force	relative positions of the subject				
declarative			**subject**	T(ense)	verb
y/n-interrogative		T	**subject**		verb
wh-interrogative	*wh*-expression	T	**subject**		verb
exclamative	*wh*-expression		**subject**	T	verb

82) Illocutionary force is the force a sentence has by being uttered by a speaker. It subsumes declarative, interrogative, imperative, and exclamative force altogether. Simply put, "illocutionary force" is equivalent to "sentential force" but felt to be a more technical term.

We may notice from the table in (44) that the pre-subject position is crucial to mark the illocutionary force of a sentence. Thus, *yes/no*-interrogative force is marked by the inverted pre-subject T, *wh*-interrogative force by the inverted *wh*-expression and T, and exclamative force by the inverted pre-subject *wh*-expression.

Strangely, however, the declarative sentence seems to have nothing to mark its force. (Note that there is nothing in its pre-subject position.) In other words, it seems to be "**unmarked**" with respect to its force. Yet, before drawing such a conclusion, let us look at the following complex sentence.

(45) [Bill knows [that three banks were robbed during the weekend]].

Needless to say, the main clause in (45) has declarative force. What about the subordinate or embedded clause?[83)] Obviously, it also has declarative force. What, then, is the role of the word *that*? To what category does it belong? Traditionally, it has been classified as a (subordinate) conjunction. But it is contrasted with other conjunctions in that it introduces a clausal complement of the main verb. Thus, it has attained the name of **complementizer (C)**.[84)] Here let us assume that besides functioning as a complementizer, *that* indicates that the clause introduced by it has declarative force. That is to say, *that* functions as a marker of declarative force.

At this point we are faced with one more question: which is

83) In (45), the main clause is surrounded by the outer pair of brackets, and the embedded one by the inner one.

84) Conjunctions other than complementizers are abbreviated as **Conj**.

the head when the complementizer *that* merges with the following clause?[85)] Previously we defined a head as what requires and selects another element. (The latter, in turn, plays the role of a complement.) Can you decide which of the two—*that* and the following clause—is the head? *That* is the head, not the following clause. *That* requires a clause and in addition it selects a finite clause, as the following data show.

(46) a. Bill knows **that** three banks *were* robbed during the weekend.
b. *Bill knows **that** three banks *to have* been robbed during the weekend.
c. *Bill knows **that** three banks *having* been robbed during the weekend.

Considering the above argument, we have every reason to represent the structure of the subordinate clause as follows.[86)]

85) Instead, you might think that the complementizer merely conjoins [*Bill knows*] and [*three banks were robbed during the weekend*] and belongs in neither side. This cannot be accepted, though. Why? In responding to this question, the following attested examples can be of help. Explain why.

(i) I will argue that the reality is more complex, and that the truth is somewhere between the three extreme positions. (Croft 2012:84)
(ii) ... and they also explained to me that there would be an hour's play and that the player who scored the fewest ten-strikes in the hour would have to provide oysters and beer for the combination. (*The Autobiography of Mark Twain*, p. 170)

86) Notice that the structure in (47) cannot be the base structure of the sentence in (46a). The reason is that the subject NP *three banks* does not originate in Spec,TP, according to the VPISH. Actually, it is taken to be moved from the object position of the verb *robbed*. Here we do not discuss its derivation in detail, since it can be rather complicated.

(47)

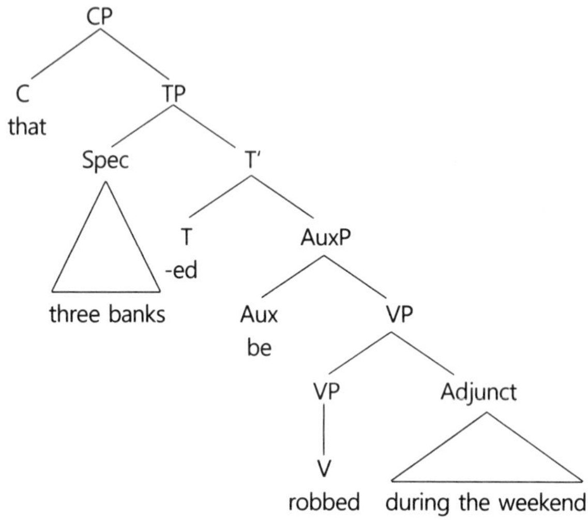

Here it would be helpful to carefully observe the **hierarchical** or **layered** structure of the sentence, paying special attention to the relative order of layering between CP, TP, AuxP, and VP. The most deeply embedded or lowest layer, VP, denotes some sort of basic event. AuxPs add meanings related to voice and/or aspect, and TP denotes the modality and/or time of the event expressed by VP. Now what about C(P)? Based upon the above analysis of the complementizer *that*, we claim that CP is the layer where illocutionary force is encoded. For instance, as we mentioned above, the complementizer *that*, as the head of CP, marks the declarative force of a subordinate clause.

What is strange is that with the declarative main clause there seems to be no illocutionary force marker visible. Nevertheless, it goes without saying that such a clause does have declarative force. Accordingly, it would be reasonable to assume that the marker of declarative force is invisible but present. Following general conventions in linguistics, let us represent the invisible force marker as ø. Our discussion leads to the following structure of the sentence in (46a).

(48)

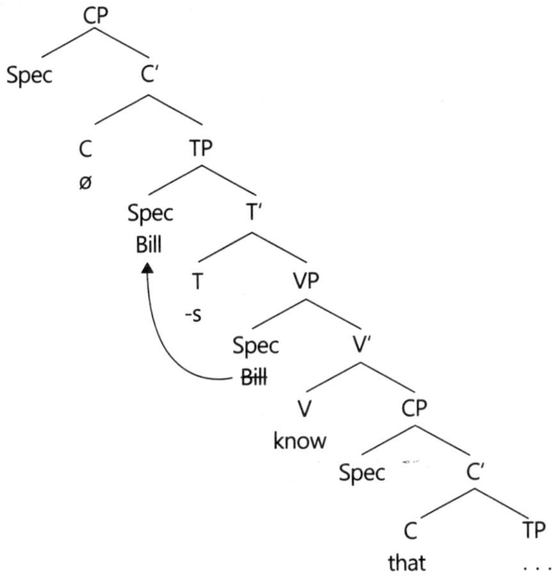

Setting aside imperative and exclamative sentences for future study, let us assume that one of the ways of encoding interrogative force is to use *if/whether* as the complementizer. The following seems to support this.

(49) Her aunt asked her {whether/if} she would make a trip to Malaysia.

Our assumption that *if/whether* marks the interrogative force of a complement clause is justified by the fact that the sentence in (49) corresponds to the following sentence containing a direct question.

(50) Her aunt said to her, "Will you make a trip to Malaysia?"

From the above discussion we may safely draw the conclusion that the CP layer is placed immediately above the TP layer and expresses the illocutionary force of a sentence or clause.

There arises a new issue, however. If we presume that the CP also contains a specifier position in conformity with the general X′ syntax format, what occupies the specifier position of CP? Before addressing this question, let us observe the summary in (44) again, and the C system, postulated in the above discussion.

(44) Illocutionary force and relative positions of the subject

illocutionary force	relative positions of the subject				
declarative			**subject**	T	verb
y/n-interrogative		T	**subject**		verb
wh-interrogative	***wh***-expression	T	**subject**		verb
exclamative	***wh***-expression		**subject**	T	verb

(51) The C system

declarative	***that/ø***	subject	T	verb
interrogative	***if/whether***	subject	T	verb

Let us focus on the elements placed in the pre-subject position. With respect to *yes/no*-questions, we hypothesized that *if/whether* acts as the marker of interrogative force in indirect questions, occupying the head C position. Now, what about direct questions?

The inverted T is likely to be equated with *if/whether*, since both —the inverted T and *if/whether*—are placed in the pre-subject position. Moreover, the following data seem to strongly support their equivalent status.

(52) a. I don't know {if/whether} he will take part in the conference.
b. *I don't know will {if/whether} he take part in the conference.
c. I asked myself, "Will he take part in the conference?"

The ungrammaticality of the sentence in (52b) shows that *will* and *if/whether* cannot occur consecutively in direct questions. Crucially, if two linguistic elements cannot occur consecutively, it is likely to be attributed to the fact that they occupy the same syntactic position. In this connection, observe the following data.

(53) a. the big cat/this big cat/*the this big cat
b. I was {extremely/greatly/*greatly extremely} surprised to hear the news.

In (53a), the third phrase is unacceptable because the two determiners—*the* and *this*—cannot be placed in the same single slot: the central determiner position. Likewise, the third alternative in (53b) is ungrammatical owing to the cooccurrence of two intensifiers in the single slot for intensifiers. Building upon these observations, we may conclude that *will* and *if/whether* in (52b) occupy the same position, that is, the head C position of CP, rendering the sentence ungrammatical.

Now, in order to answer the question of what occupies the

Spec,CP, let us turn to *wh*-questions. Given below is a typical example.

(54) (=(38Ba) What did he buy in Europe?

The *wh*-question in (54) is supposed to undergo the following derivational process in the light of the discussion so far.

(55)

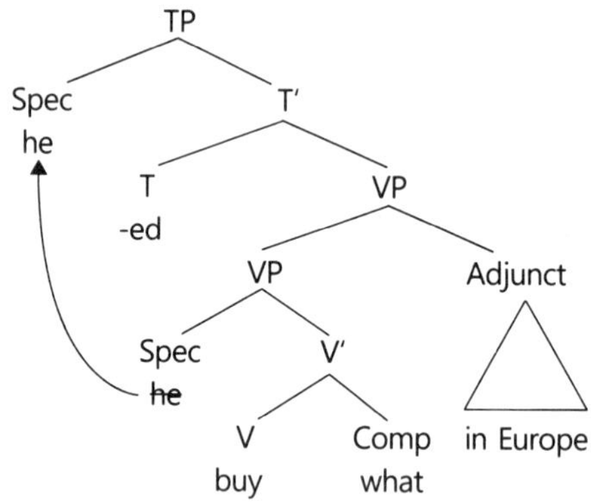

However, the structure in (55) appears to be lacking in something. What do you suppose it is? It lacks a means for expressing interrogative force, and therefore it does not look different at all from the structure of the corresponding declarative sentence. This implies that its semantics is almost identical with that of the latter, an undesirable consequence.

Incidentally, given that illocutionary force of a sentence is marked by the C head, there should be at least four kinds of C heads: the declarative C, interrogative C, imperative C, and exclamative C. As we discussed in the foregoing, in the case of subordinate complement clauses, the declarative and interrogative Cs are marked by *that* and *if/whether*, respectively. On the other hand, in the case of main clauses, there seem to be no visible distinctive Cs to mark the four types of illocutionay force. For the purpose of the present discussion, let us differentiate the four types of C heads by using the following feature system.

(56) Feature system for distinguishing the four types of C head[87)]

a. the declarative C: C
[dec]

b. the interrogative C: C
[int]

c. the imperative C: C
[imp]

d. the exclamative C: C
[exc]

By adopting the above feature system, we can distinctively represent the base structure for the sentence in (54) and that for the corresponding declarative sentence as follows.

87) [dec], [int], [imp], and [exc] are abbreviations for [declarative], [interrogative], [imperative], and [exclamative], respectively.

(57)

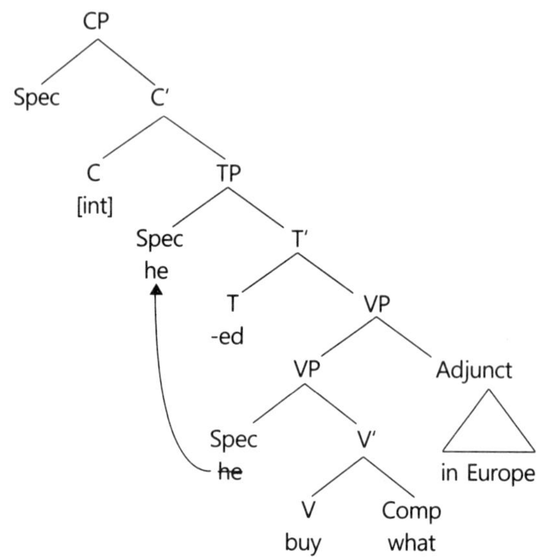

(58)

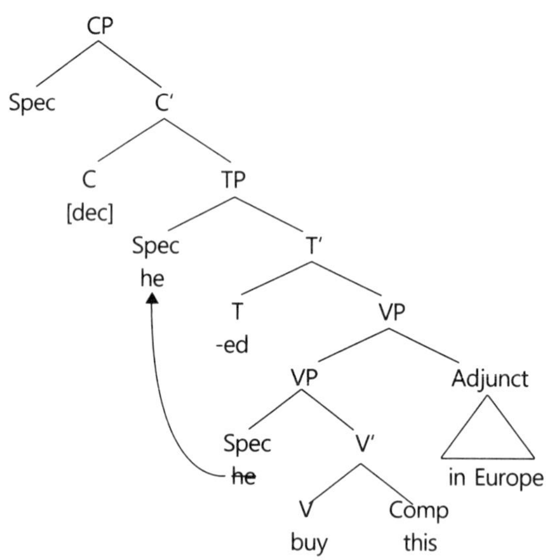

Although the two representations are truly differentiated by use of the "invisible" distinctive features [int] and [dec], the lingering problem is that they are not "visibly" differentiated on the surface. Here we claim that the movement of T to C occurs to *visibly* differentiate the interrogative C from the declarative one or to mark interrogative force visibly. In other words, the "invisible" feature [int] in C triggers the movement. Remarkably, the *wh*-expression is also induced to move, filling the Spec,CP, as can be seen in the following structure.

(59)

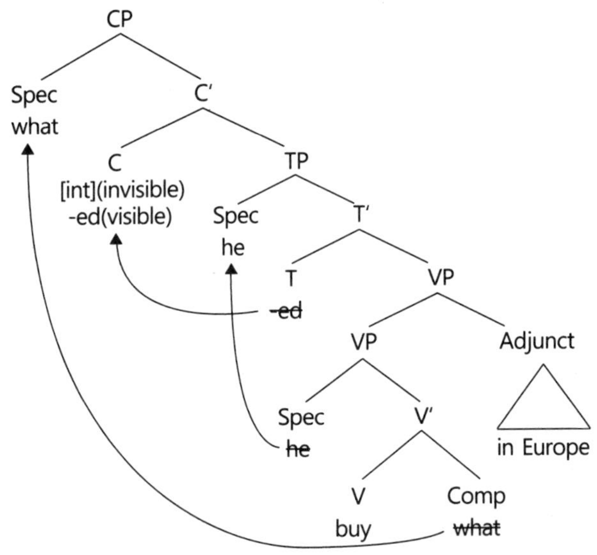

Another noticeable thing in (59) is the stranded suffix *-ed*. As was noted earlier, it cannot stand alone, and must be attached to a verb, since it is a verbal suffix. In English, verb raising is disallowed. Nor can *-ed* lower onto the verb *buy*, since it has been moved to the C head position in order to mark interrogative force. We can rescue the stranded *-ed* by means of *do*-support, which results in the structure in (60).

(60)

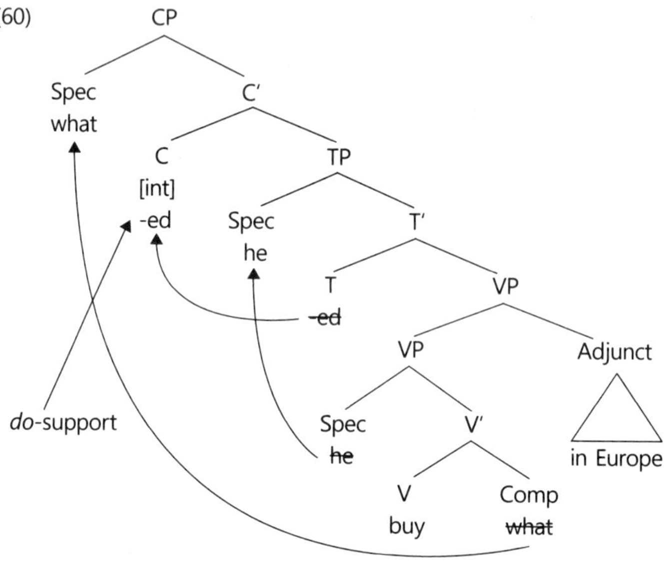

Do-ed is spelt out as *did*, producing this sentence: *What did he buy in Europe*?

Now I expect that you are fairly well acquainted with the generative approach to structural analyses of basic sentences in English. In the next section, we will end our discussion on the syntactic structures of English sentences by presenting a canonical analysis of the *students* sentence and its *wh*-interrogative analogue. In the course of the final analysis you will review all the lessons you have learned concerning the syntactic analysis of English sentences throughout this book.

5.7 A canonical analysis of the two sentences

At the beginning of the present textbook, we set up its goal: to analyze the *students* sentence and its somewhat enriched *wh*-interrogative counterpart. Observe the following sentences that are further enriched based upon the two sentences for the purpose of discussion.

(61) These students of English history will be visiting the British Museum on the second Tuesday of May.

(62) When do you think that the students of English history will visit the British Museum?

Mindful of the process of syntactic analysis expounded throughout this book, let us try to analyze the given sentences.

First of all, the first sentence consists of seventeen **words**, so it is said to contain the seventeen **smallest constituents**. Second, let us try to detect larger constituents than words. Aside from the constituents containing the verb head *visiting*, we can identify the following: *These students of English history*, *the British Museum*, *on the second Tuesday of May*. Needless to say, the three constituents are not the second smallest constituents, since they contain one or more constituents larger than words. At any rate, we have to offer some justifications for our judgment that each of the three is a constituent. It should not be difficult if you have understood what a constituent is and acquainted yourself with the **diagnostics for identifying constituents**. For instance, we can show that each of the three strings of words forms a constituent, by adding the following sentence to the sentence in (1).

(63) Their professors recommended that they visit it then.

In the sentence in (63) what do the underlined proforms refer to? *They* is substituted for *These students of English history*, *it* is substituted for *the British Museum*, and *then* replaces *on the second Tuesday of May*. Thus, the **substitutability test** proves that all the three strings of words are constituents.

Now we need to investigate the internal structure of each of them. In the case of *These students of English history*, the head of the overall phrase is *students*, since that is the semantic core. Based upon the word class of *students*, we classify the whole phrase as NP. At this stage, we analyze the NP by matching it with the X′ syntax format. The results are: *These* is the specifier of the NP, and *of English history* is its complement. (Note that the relationship between *students* and *of English history* is identical with that between the verb *study* and its object *English history*, which justifies our assignment of the complement status to *of English history*. This can be represented by the following tree diagram.

(64)

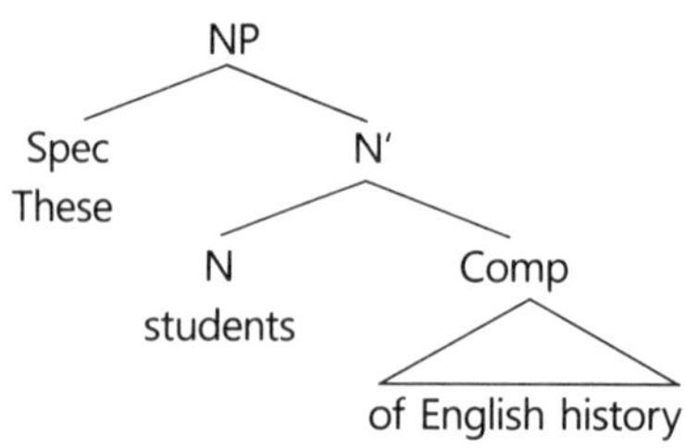

It is evident from the above tree diagram that the present analysis is not exhaustive. The complement *of English history* is not analyzed at all. However, its analysis is straightforward. The head is the preposition *of* (on what grounds?), and *English history* is the complement. Consequently, the category of *of English history* is PP, and its functional status is the complement of *students*. What about *English history*? Evidently, it is an NP, since its head is *history*. The final analysis we have reached is as follows. (Note that every phrase constitutes a three-level projection, even if it consists of only one word. For this reason, non-existence of a specifier or a complement is taken as existence of a zero specifier or a zero complementizer.)

(65)

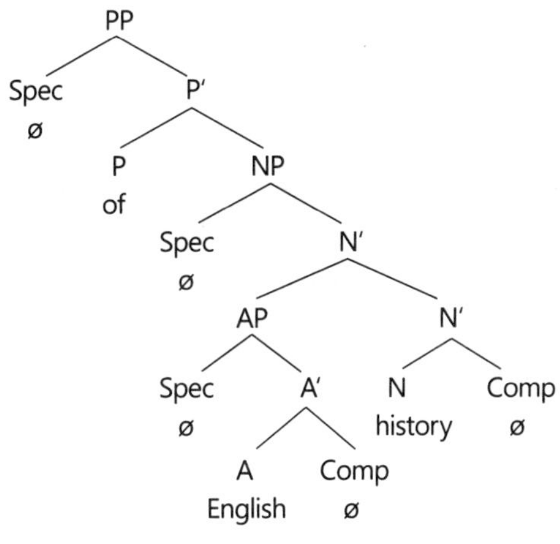

What about *the British Museum* and *on the second Tuesday of May*? The structure of the former is very simple: it is an NP with the specifier *the* and the adjunct *British*. As for the latter, it is relatively complex. The head of the whole phrase is the preposition *on*, which takes the NP *the second Tuesday of May* as its complement. The NP's head is *Tuesday*, as it is the semantic core. Since the typical specifier of NP is a determiner, we assign the specifier status to *the.* In the case of *second* and *of May* it is not unreasonable to classify them as adjuncts, since they modify the head. Considering that *of May* seems to be semantically closer to *Tuesday* than *second* is,[88] let us assume that the former merges with *Tuesday* prior to the latter. The results of our analysis so far are captured by the following two tree diagrams.

(66)

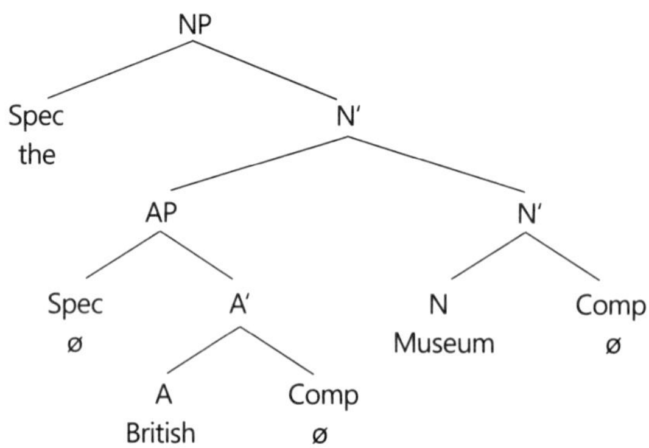

88) The meaning of *the second Tuesday of May* is 'the second of the four or five Tuesdays of May' rather than 'the second Tuesday of May of the many second Tuesdays (in a year).'

(67)

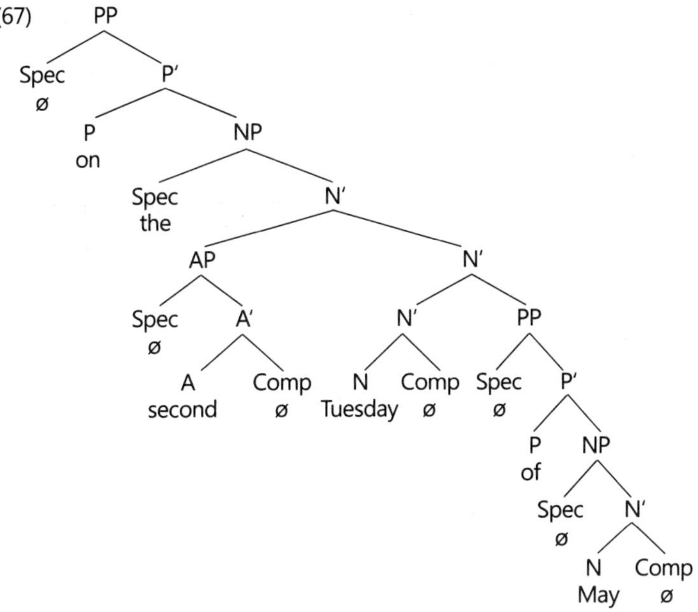

However, drawing tree diagrams in detail everytime would be bothersome. Accordingly, in the current syntactic literature, somewhat simplified diagrams are used. For instance, the diagram in (65) can be simplified as follows.

(65')

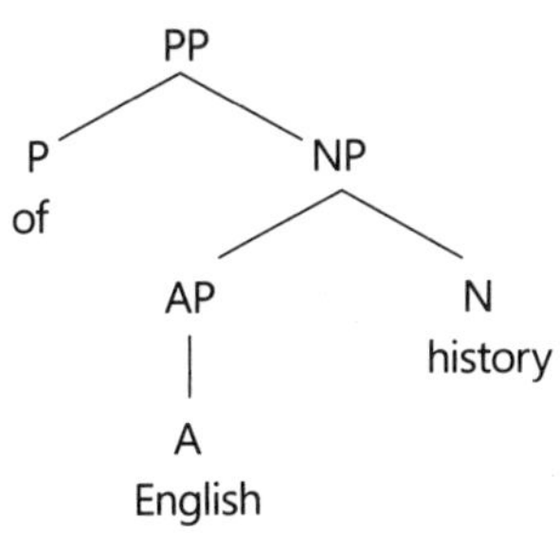

A rule of thumb for simplification is this: first, give every word its (lexical) category; second, when two words or constituents are

merged, give the non-projecting, that is, non-head constituent its maximal projection, omitting its intermediate projection; third, intermediate projections are represented only if all the three projections (X-X′-XP) are relevant; fourth, do not represent zero (ø) constituents. If we follow this rule, we can simplify the tree diagrams in (66)-(67) as follows.[89]

(66′)

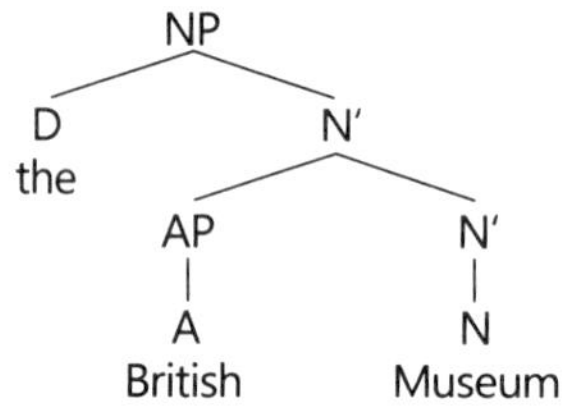

(67′)[90]

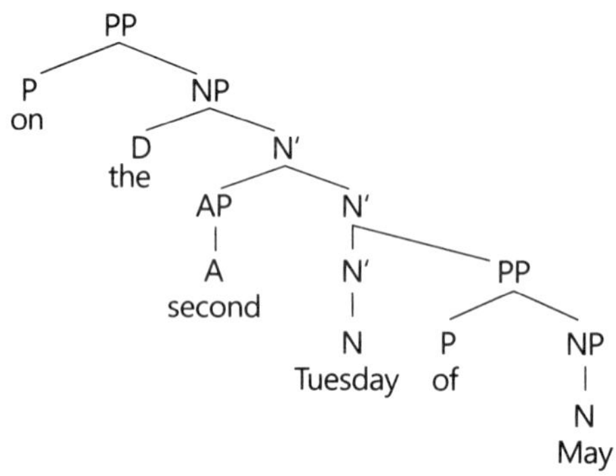

89) Some might argue that of the two N′s in (66′) the lower one is unnecessary. However, if we omit it, we cannot differentiate an adjunct from a complement. Note that adjuncts merge with X′/XP, generating another X′/XP, while complements and specifiers take X and X′, generating X′ and XP, respectively.

90) Two things are worthy of note concerning the tree diagram in (67′). First, the category D is peculiar in that it does not abide by the previously mentioned rule of thumb. It does not project, but is not labeled as DP. Secondly, the lowest N′ is used for capturing the adjunct status of the PP *of May*. For the resolution of the peculiarity of the category D, Abney (1987) proposed the **DP hypothesis**. This book is intended for undergraduate students, and we neither discuss, nor adopt, the DP hypothesis.

Now that we have completed the analysis of the three main constituents, we turn to the verb and constituents formed around it. Needless to say, the verb *visiting* functions as the head of the VP. More specifically, it is a transitive verb, and accordingly it requires an object. In addition, it requires an NP to which it can assign the agent role (i.e., the visitor role). These requirements of the verb are satisfied by the successive mergers of the verb with the object, and with the subject, which result in a VP projection in the wake of the X′ format, as can be seen in the following representation.

(68)

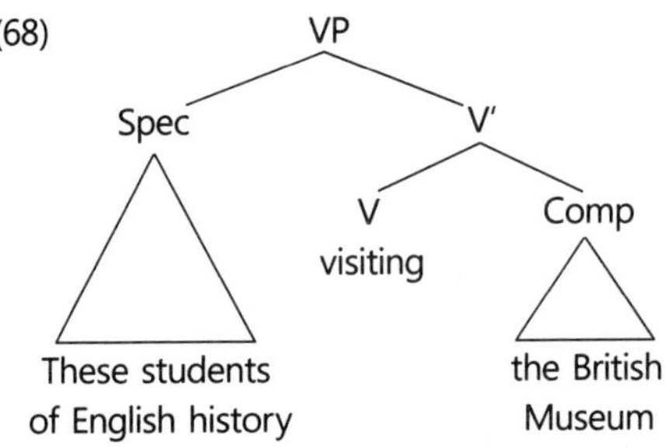

Adjoined to this structure is the adjunct *on the second Tuesday of May*, expanding the VP further. Successive mergers adding the progressive *be* and the T head *will* result in this pre-final structure.

(69)

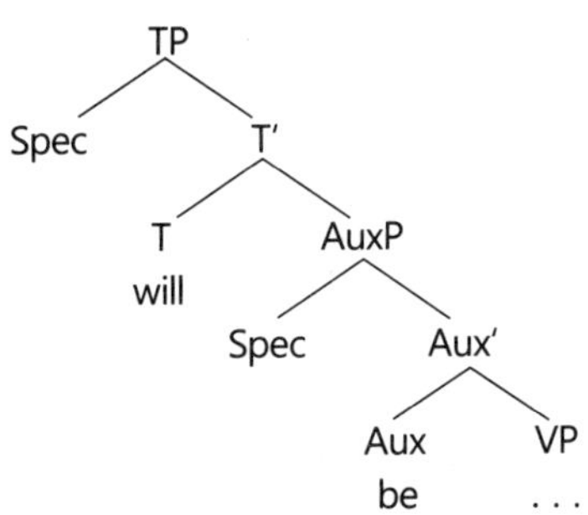

At the final stage of derivation, the EPP triggers the movement of the subject in Spec,VP to Spec,TP. As we showed in section 5.5, the subject stops by every intervening specifier position. The final structure we arrive at is the following. (For space reasons, we cannot provide the detailed internal structures for the specifier, the complement, and the adjunct. See (64)-(67) and (65')-(67').)

(70)[91]

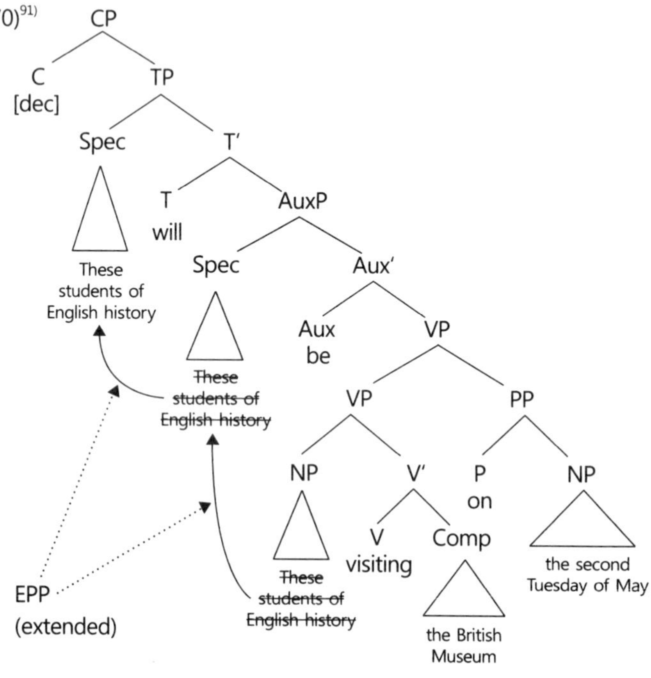

In deriving the above structure from the words selected from the lexicon we use two kinds of syntactic operations: **merge** and **move**. The operation merge is executed such that only two elements are

91) Note that the tree diagram contains categorial as well as functional labels. This inconsistency might seem strange, but is usual in the literature.

allowed to merge at a time. That is, merger of more than two elements at a time is not allowed in human language.[92)]

What we need to note concerning the operation move is that the subject in Spec,VP does not move to Spec,TP, its final destination, at one fell swoop, but in a step-by-step fashion. Thus, it stops in every intervening specifier position, which justifies the postulation of Spec,AuxP and enables us to unify all sorts of phrases by means of the X′ syntax format.

Let us now turn to the second sentence, which can be considered a typical example of *wh*-questions. Observe the following data, which contain an additional example of *wh*-question for discussion.

(71) What did he want?

(72) When do you think that the students of English history will visit the British Museum?

In section 5.4, we showed that sentences like that in (71) are derived by *wh*-movement. More concretely, its derivational process is represented as follows.

---

92) The **BMP** is known to apply in phonology and morphology as well. Note the following representations showing the binary-branching phonological and morphological structure.

(i)

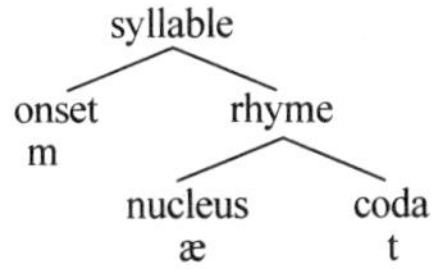

(ii)

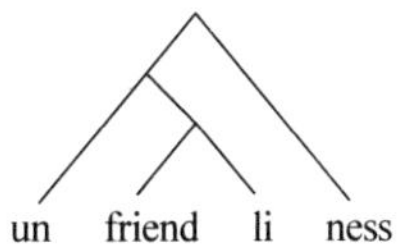

(73)

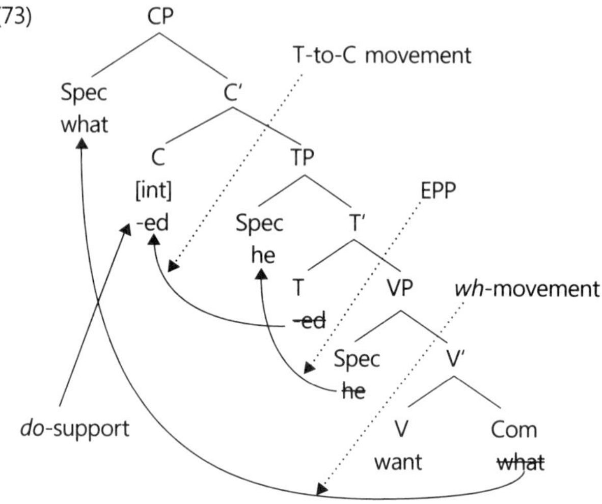

Now, how do we account for the derivation of the sentence in (72)? At a glance it may seem to be a garden-variety *wh*-question, but it raises some issues about our analysis of *wh*-questions. First, where does the *wh*-word *when* originate? If we are asked the question in (72), we are likely to answer by saying, for instance,

(74) I think that they will visit it next Wednesday.

This leads us to claim that *when,* though placed in the sentence-initial position, originated in the embedded clause as the adjunct of the VP *visit the British Museum* and has moved to Spec,CP in the main clause.

The above argument for our analysis is conceptual. Our analysis will become more robust if we secure empirical argument as well. Is there any empirical evidence supporting our claim? Confronted with a similar question pertaining to the movement of the subject, we presented sentences containing a floating quantifier as empirical supporting evidence, for instance:

(75) a. *All* the boys have been playing together on the playground.
  b. The boys have *all* been playing together on the playground.
  c. The boys have been *all* playing together on the playground.

The locations of *all* indicate the places through which the subject has passed in the course of derivation of the sentence.

In a parallel way, it would be worthwhile to try to collect some examples concerned with the *wh*-movement that leaves something behind. Fortunately, there are relevant examples like the following.

(76) a. What *all* did you get for Christmas?
  b. What did you get *all* for Christmas?
  c. What *all* did John say that Peter ate for breakfast?
  d. What did John say that Peter ate *all* for breakfast?

(Boeckx 2006:170)

From a semantic viewpoint, *what* and *all* must form a constituent. It is natural, therefore, that they move together. But as noted by Boeckx, "*all* can be left behind in intermediate steps of movement, acting like footprints, identifying a position targeted by movement" as well as the position it originates in. Thus, it is evident from the above data that *what* has moved from the object position of the verbs *get* and *ate*. This observation is sufficient to empirically support our claim that in (72) *when* is moved from an adjunct position of the VP in the subordinate clause.

An additional question posed concerning the *wh*-question in (72) is how *when* has moved to Spec,CP of the main clause. Has it moved at one fell swoop, or has it dropped in (an) intermediate place(s), if any? If it has moved in a step-by-step fashion, where has it dropped in? There seems to be no theoretical motivation for preference for either of the two. In this connection, *wh*-movements occurring with something stranded would play a crucial role in choosing one over the other. Observe the following relevant data.[93)]

(77) a. What *exactly* did he say that he wanted?
b. What did he say that he wanted *exactly*?
c. What did he say *exactly* that he wanted?

Exactly in (77b) shows that *what* has moved from the object position of the verb *wanted*. What is striking is the fact that *exactly* can also be stranded to the left of the complementizer *that,* as evidenced by the sentence in (77c). Now, precisely what position does this stranded *exactly* occupy? In other words, what is the category label of the location of *exactly* in (77c)? There are two possibilities. It can be either the object position of the verb *say* or the specifier position of the CP headed by the complementizer *that*. Which do you think it is? The former is implausible since *what exactly* is the object of the verb *wanted*, not the verb *say*. The object of *say* is the whole clause introduced by *that*. Hence, obviously, *(what) exactly* is placed in the specifier position of the

93) Every moved element leaves behind an invisible unpronounced copy. If we represent the copies left behind with strikethrough, we obtain the following, as shown in Haegeman 2006:338.

(i) a. What exactly did he say ~~what exactly~~ that he wanted ~~what exactly~~?
b. What did he say ~~what~~ that he wanted ~~what~~ exactly?
c. What did he say ~~what~~ exactly that he wanted ~~what exactly~~?

CP headed by *that*. To conclude our argumentation so far, the sentence in (72) is derived as follows.

(78) Derivational Process of (72)[94)]

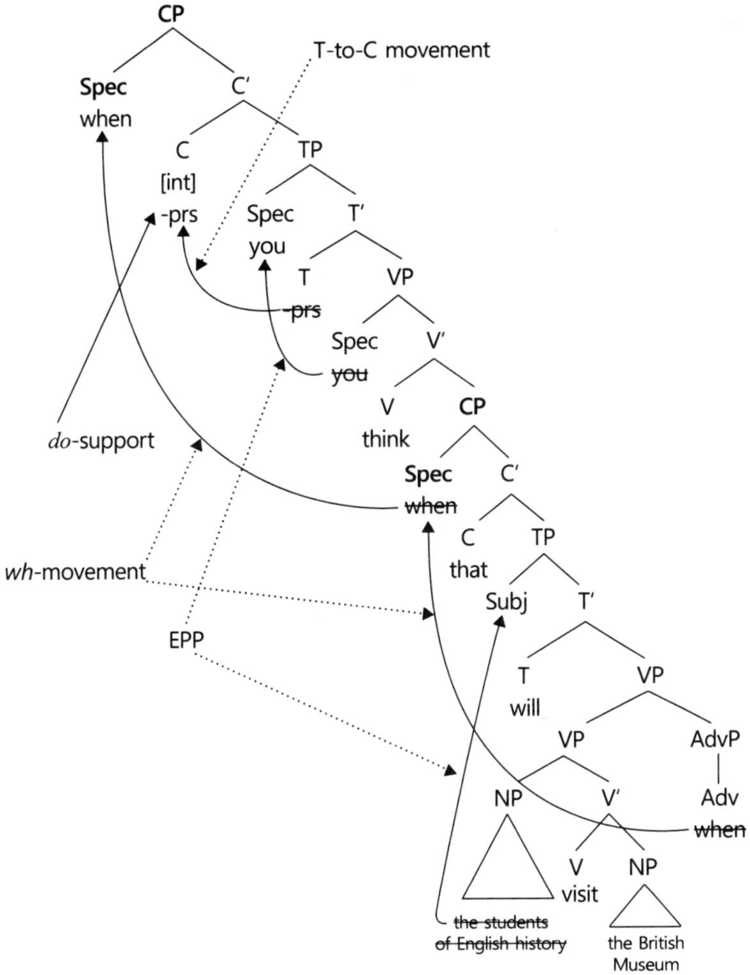

94) For space reasons, we replace the phrase *the students of English history* with Subj in the Spec,TP in the embedded clause.

What must be noted from the above discussion as well as the above derivation is that *wh*-expressions like *when* move to their (final) **landing site**, i.e., the highest Spec,CP, stopping by every intermediate Spec,CP. Syntacticians call this **successive cyclic movement**. Why *wh*-movement behaves like this is one of the problems we have to solve in future study.

Needless to say, this is not the whole story of English syntax. Rather, we have only dealt with a small fraction of it from the perspective of generative theory of syntax. What I hope is that readers of this book have become interested in English syntax. Interested readers are referred to syntax textbooks like Radford 2004, 2009, Hornstein, *et. al*. 2005 as well as many other references cited there.

Exercise 1 Draw a tree diagram for representing the base structure of the sentences in (36). In addition, show how each of them is derived from the base structure. Needless to say, you should include the specifier positions for all the phrases.

Exercise 2 Show how the sentences in (1) and (2) are derived and explain how the data below are taken to support the VPISH.

(1) a. *All* the boys seem to appear to like ice cream.
    b. The boys seem *all* to appear to like ice cream.
    c. The boys seem to appear *all* to like ice cream.
    d. The boys seem to appear to *all* like ice cream.
(Boeckx 2006:170)

(2) a. The students should have been *all* doing the exam at that time.
    b. The students should have *all* been doing the exam at that time.
    c. The students should *all* have been doing the exam at that time.
(Haegeman 2006:269)

(3) We *all* want to take part but we don't necessarily *all* know how and where. (BBC radio 4, Oct. 29, 2002)

(4) But it has not *all* been easy. (*Guardian* Nov. 22, 2002)

(5) We cannot *all* drive into a city. (*Guardian* Nov. 22, 2002)
((3)-(5) are adopted from Haegeman 2006)

Exercise 3 State what illocutionary force each clause contained in the following has and draw a tree diagram for each sentence, including the features for representing the illocutionary force.

(1) David loved Jane.
(2) David wondered where Jane was born.
(3) McDavid exclaimed what a nice party he had last Saturday.
(4) Did you believe that he told a lie to his father?

Exercise 4 Show how the following example can be used to argue that adverbs merge later than the subject in a VP.

(1) The dragons simply all died out. (Adger 2003:209)

Exercise 5 How can you justify the analyses in footnote 92?

Exercise 6 Surprisingly, the tree diagram in (14) on page 18 violates the BMP. This cannot be treated as an exception, because every coordinated phrase poses the same problem. How can we solve this problem?

References

(Those mentioned in the preface are included.)

Aarts, Bas. 1997. *English syntax and argumentation.* New York: Palgrave.

Aarts, Bas. 2001. *English syntax and argumentation.* 2nd ed. New York: Palgrave.

Aarts, Bas. 2011. *Oxford modern English grammar*. Oxford: Oxford University Press.

Abney, Steven P. 1987. *The English noun phrase in its sentential aspect.* Doctoral dissertation, MIT.

Adger, David. 2003. *Core syntax: A minimalist approach.* Oxford: Oxford University Press.

Akmajian, Adrian, and Frank Heny. 1975. *An introduction to the principles of transformational syntax*. Cambridge, Mass.: MIT Press.

Bloomfield, Leonard. 1933. *Language*. Boston: George Allen & Unwin.

Boeckx, Cedric. 2006. *Linguistic minimalism: Origins, concepts, methods, and aims*. Oxford: Oxford University Press.

Bolinger, Dwight. 1977. *Meaning and form*. London: Longman.

Carnie, Andrew. 2002. *Syntax: A generative introduction.* Oxford: Blackwell.

Carnie, Andrew. 2013. *Syntax: A generative introduction.* 3rd ed. Malden, Mass.: Wiley-Blackwell.

Chomsky, Noam. 1957. *Syntactic structures*. The Hague: Mouton.

Chomsky, Noam. 1965. *Aspects of the theory of syntax*. Cambridge, Mass.:MIT Press.

Chomsky, Noam. 1995. *The minimalist program.* Cambridge, Mass.: MIT Press.

Croft, William. 2012. *Verbs: aspect and causal structure*. Oxford: Oxford University Press.

Einstein, Albert. 1954. *Ideas and opinions*. Translated by Sonja Bragmann. New York: Dell Publishers.

Fillmore, Charles. 1968. The case for case. In Emmon Bach and Robert T. Harms, eds. *Universals in linguistic theory*, 1-90 New York: Holt, Rinehart, Winston.

Greenbaum, Sidney, and Gerald Nelson. 2009. *An introduction to English grammar*. 3rd ed. New York: Pearson Education.

Griffiths, James, and Mark de Vries. 2013. The syntactic integration of appositives: Evidence from fragments and ellipsis. *Linguistic Inquiry* 44:332-344.

Gruber, Jeffrey S. 1965. *Studies in lexical relations*. Doctoral dissertation, MIT.

Haegeman, Liliane. 1991. *Introduction to government and binding theory*. Oxford: Blackwell.

Haegeman, Liliane. 2006. *Thinking syntactically: A guide to argumentation and analysis*. Malden, Mass.: Blackwell.

Hornstein, Norbert, Jairo Nunes, and Kleanthes K. Grohmann. 2005. *Understanding minimalism*. Cambridge: Cambridge University Press.

Huddleston, Rodney and Geoffrey K. Pullum. 2002. *The Cambridge grammar of the English language*. Cambridge: Cambridge University Press.

Jackendoff, Ray. 1972. *Semantic interpretation in generative grammar*. Cambridge, Mass.: MIT Press.

Jespersen, Otto. 1933. *Essentials of English grammar*. London: George Allen and Unwin.

Kearns, Kate. 2000. *Semantics*. London: Macmillan Press.

Mark Twain. 1990. *The autobiography of Mark Twain*. Edited by Charles Neider. New York: HarperPerennial.

McCawley, James D. 1988. *The syntactic phenomena of English*. Chicago: University of Chicago Press

Palmer, Frank. 1990. *Modality and the English modals*. 2nd ed. London: Longman.

Postal, Paul M. 1974. *On raising: One rule of English grammar and its theoretical implications*. Cambridge, Mass.: MIT Press.

Pyles, Thomas and John Algeo. 1993. *The origins and development of the English language*. 4th ed. New York: Harcourt Brace Jovanovich.

Quirk, Randolph, Sidney Greenbaum, Geoffrey Leech, and Jan Svartvik. 1985. *A comprehensive grammar of the English language*. London: Longman.

Radford, Andrew. 1988. *Transformational grammar: A first course*. Cambridge: Cambridge University Press.

Radford, Andrew. 2004. *English syntax: An introduction.* Cambridge: Cambridge University Press.

Radford, Andrew. 2009. *Analyzing English sentences: A minimalist approach.* Cambridge: Cambridge University Press.

Reinhart, Tanya. 1976. *The syntactic domain of anaphora.* Doctoral dissertation, MIT.

Reinhart, Tanya. 1983. *Anaphora and semantic interpretation.* Chicago: University of Chicago Press.

Reuland, Eric. 2011. *Anaphora and language design.* Cambridge, Mass.: MIT Press.

Ross, John Robert. 1967. *Constraints on variables in syntax.* Doctoral dissertation, MIT.

Ross, John Robert. 1986. *Infinite syntax.* Norwood, N.J. : Ablex.

Sandel, Michael J. 2009. *Justice: What's the right thing to do?* New York: Farrar, Straus and Giroux.

Saussure, Ferdinand de. 1959. *Course in general linguistics.* Edited by Charles Bally and Albert Reidlinger and Translated from the French by Wade Baskin. New York: Philosophical Library.

Soams, Scott, and David M. Perlmutter. 1979. *Syntactic argumentation and the structure of English.* Los Angeles: University of California Press.

Wierzbicka, Anna. 1988. *The semantics of grammar.* Amsterdam: John Benjamins.

Index

김성욱

서울대 영어교육과 (학사)
서울대 대학원 영어영문학과 (석사, 박사)
(현) 충북대 영어영문학과 교수

English Syntax

An Introduction to Generative Theory

초판 1쇄 발행 _ 2014년 12월 31일

저 자 • 김 성 욱
발 행 인 • 정 현 걸
발 행 • 신 아 사
인 쇄 • 예지인쇄
출판등록 • 1956년 1월 5일 (제9-52호)
주 소 • 서울특별시 은평구 녹번동 28-36번지 2F
전 화 • (02)382-6411 • 팩스 (02)382-6401
홈페이지 • www.shinasa.co.kr
E-MAIL • shinasa@daum.net

ISBN: 978-89-8396-878-4 (93740)

정가 12,000원